WRECKERS

Commissioned and first performe[...] one of our foremost political theatre groups, [...] Edgar's first piece since the award-winning *Destiny*.

A play with music, **Wreckers** tells the story of various crimes and various kinds of criminal. Set in the East End, the first half contrasts the imprisonment of the five dockers under the Industrial Relations Act 1972 with some murkier goings-on in the London Rag Trade. The second half takes the same characters forward four years to 1976 and traces their involvement in a left-wing 'takeover' of a constituency Labour Party in an effort to oust the local MP.

Written with his customary wit and attack, Edgar's new play demonstrates once again his talent for expressing complex political issues in a way that is at the same time dramatic, provocative and highly entertaining.

7:84

7:84 Theatre Company began in 1971, and since then has toured extensively in England, Scotland, Wales, Ireland and Holland. In 1973 the Company developed into two separate companies – 7:84 Scotland and 7:84 England.

Their aim is to provide good entertainment, music and theatre for ordinary working people in clubs, community centres, theatres and halls – anywhere people want to go, and can afford to go, for a night out. Over the last five years they have performed to hundreds of thousands of people – and travelled almost as many miles.

The Company work as part of the Labour Movement, setting out to provide something familiar in entertainment value but different in what it's saying: to provide the best of entertainment for working people through the presentation of shows which have a direct relevance to their lives. Most people have never been encouraged to see theatre as anything but entertainment for an elite. 7:84 are trying to help change that image.

WRECKERS

DAVID EDGAR

A Methuen New Theatrescript
Eyre Methuen · London

To Chris Parr

First published in 1977 by Eyre Methuen Ltd, 11 New Fetter Lane,
London EC4P 4EE
Copyright © 1977 by David Edgar
Music copyright © 1977 by the individual composers or their publishers
Printed in Great Britain by Expression Printers Ltd, London

ISBN 0 413 38510 8

Introduction

Wreckers was written with and for the 7:84 Company England, but the show is not exclusive to 7:84, and could most certainly be performed by others. It is useful though, I think, for both the general reader and any potential presenter of the play to know how this script came into being.

7:84 is a collective company of performers, musicians, technicians and administrators, which employs out-workers (directors, designers and writers) for individual shows. The company acknowledges the individual skills of both in- and out-workers, but believes that the pursuit of specific crafts should follow the widest possible discussion and debate within the group as a whole.

This show began with lengthy discussions between the group, the director Penny Cherns, and me. There was a strong feeling that the show should be about the law, both in its application and basic character. Out of this came the idea of a play set in the London Docks, which would deal with criminal law, with industrial law, and, finally, with the nature of Parliamentary legislation as a whole.

Having decided on the subject and agreed an outline, we researched the show, everyone reading round the subject, and conducting interviews collectively. (In more than parenthesis, we'd like to thank the many people we did interview; including Sean Barrett, Andy Bevan, Ben Birnbaum, Alex Dunn, Maggie Foy, Ian Olley and Pat Olley; the Joint Docklands Action Committee; Colin Chambers of the *Morning Star* and Bob Light and Jimmy Clark of *The Dockworker*: they helped us get many things right, though we, of course, are responsible for what's wrong.) At the end of the research period, I produced another outline, which was discussed and amended. I then went away to write the script, returning some weeks later with a draft, which was extensively re-written during its five-week rehearsal. This book is the text that resulted from that process, and there are aspects of it that are specific to this production.

First, casting. 7:84 is blessed with a company of six performers, some of whom play instruments, and four musicians, all of whom play parts. The doubling used in **Wreckers** resulted from this happy circumstance: the play could be done, however, with a non-performing band, and one extra male performer.

Second, the songs. Some of the numbers were written for specific characters, others (often narrative or commentary songs) were performed by those available. Because this depended, often, on the particular requirements of this production, I have left some of the songs unspecified.

Finally, a point about the process of making **Wreckers**. There is a rather cynical argument that the kind of collective processes we employed are little more than a co-operative cosmetic for traditional, hierarchical methods of work, and that companies should either go the whole hog (and write, direct and design as a group), or go no hog at all. Certainly, real collectivity is hard work. There is a conflict between the individual skill and the general will, and group discussions often can (and did) prove unbearably tortuous, circuitous and frustrating.

However, in the end, I believe that this is the most rewarding and genuinely creative way of making a show: and that the experience on this show proved it. All the virtues of the text came out of our method of work; its failings are caused not by too much democracy, but too little.

David Edgar

Characters

GEORGE, a detective
RACHEL, a garment worker
MICKY, a docker
HUDI, a lorry-driver
LINDA, a garment worker
ANNA, a student
MORRIS, a garment trade employer
MISS JONES, a buyer
A MINER
DON, a stevedore
WPC RAYNOR, a policewoman
ANGEL, an underground railway station
A MEMBER of Parliament
GEORGE, a reporter
PAUL, an extremist
MRS WILLIS, a moderate
BERNIE, a chairperson
A RECEPTIONIST
An ANGRY MAN
A Party SECRETARY

PICKETS, RECRUITEES, GARMENT WORKERS and a BAND

Wreckers was first presented by the 7:84 Company England at the Barnfield Theatre, Exeter on 10 February 1977 with the following cast:

Jim Barclay	George, Morris, Don, Member
Mike Barton	Bass Guitar, Violin, Bernie, Angel
Johnny Mulcahy	Micky, Paul
Chrissie Cotterill	Rachel, Receptionist
Si Cowe	Guitars, Mandolin, Secretary
Eddie Leach	Percussion, Angry Man
Mike O'Neill	Keyboards, Miner
Vari Sylvester	Anna, Miss Jones, WPC Raynor
Harriet Walter	Linda, Mrs Willis, Flute
Gareth Williams	Hudi, Bass Guitar
Mark Brown	Vocal arrangements
Penny Cherns	Direction
Nicola Gill	Wardrobe assistant
Gemma Jackson	Design assistant
Mike Newton	Poster design
Nick Redgrave	Set and prop maker
Di Seymour	Design and costumes
Sue Timothy	Administration
Alan Tweedie	Local liaison and publicity
Mike Vowles	Stage Management
Nigel Walker	Lighting

The music for the songs was composed by Mike Barton, Si Cowe, Mike O'Neill, Harriet Walter and Gareth Williams.

ACT ONE

"It shall be an unfair industrial practice for any person, in contemplation or furtherance of an industrial dispute, to induce or threaten to induce another person to break a contract to which the other person is a party."

Clause 96,
The Industrial Relations Act 1971

"The issue is whether these men are to be allowed to opt out of the rule of law. Can they pick and choose, relying on it for the protection of their homes and families, but rejecting it when, even temporarily, it obstructs their industrial objectives? It's a very simple issue, but vastly important, for our whole way of life is based upon the acceptance of the rule of law."

Sir John Donaldson,
on his imprisonment of five dockers,
21 July 1972

"There is a sense in which all law is nothing more nor less than a gigantic confidence trick. Law is not enforceable at all if a sufficient number of people disregard it, and this is true of all laws."

Lord Hailsham,
12 April 1972

ACT ONE

Scene One

Enter GEORGE *in a spot. He wears a raincoat. He smokes a cigarette. He speaks to the audience.*

GEORGE: OK. The prologue. Fill you in.
Time: 1972. Edward Heath is Prime Minister. Harold Wilson is leader of the Opposition. The Queen is the Queen.
Place: The East End. London's Gangland. Where force rules the frightened streets, only might is right, and if G. Davis is innocent OK, that sets him apart from 90 per cent of the population.
Subject of story: Conspiracies of various kinds to undermine our Way of Life and Cherished Liberties.
And I, for the time being, am George. Occupation: Detective Sergeant in the Metropolitan Constabulary. The Force. London's Finest. The Boys in Blue. Or, as they call us round here, the Filth.

Into first song:

The Filth*

SONG:
The Filth
The Filth

We are here to tell you of our role
We are guardians of the law
(And that's our trade)
We are here to serve you as a whole
Whether you are rich or poor
(On legal aid)
Riding round the manor
In our Z-Car or our panda
Or our bike
We observe a felon
Nick an orange or a lemon
And we strike

Chorus:
We are the boys in blue
And our aim it is to serve
Some say we're bent, not true
Well, perhaps a little curved

---

*Music for all the songs is at the end of the book.

The Filth
The Filth

We will always tell the court the Truth
Well, we always tell the time
(Well, now and then)
We are quite devoid of any ruth
In our hot pursuit of crime
(It's half past ten)
If you come a cropper
Call your friendly local copper
He won't mind
After due inspection
He will give you his protection
All the time

Chorus
The Filth
The Filth

Scene Two

During the song, a pub has been set up. A table and four chairs. At the end of the song, GEORGE *comes forward again.*

GEORGE: It is January 1972. Unemployment is nudging a million and the Stock Exchange index is nudging 500. Inflation is over seven per cent and the pound is sinking below two dollars sixty. And it's a Friday night in a public hostelry on the Isle of Dogs, the kind of place where even the cat backs the Hammers, and you can't bung a brick without braining half a dozen colourful East End characters.

Enter RACHEL. *She stands.*

Rachel Carter. Five foot six. Eyes, blue. Stated occupation: Presser in the garment industry. She was a tough cookie, but, then, she'd had a disturbed childhood. She used to pick her spots and bite her nails. When she grew up, she moved on to rivets.

RACHEL *sits. Enter* MICKY, *with two pints. He stands.*

Micky Carter. Five foot ten. Eyes green. Stated occupation: docker in the Royal Group. His easy-going, happy-go-lucky exterior concealed the fact that his interior was just the same.

MICKY *sits. Enter* HUDI *with a pint*

and a half. He stands.

And Gerry Neill, known as Hudi. Two inch heels, bloodshot, highly dubious. He was known as a joker. That's because people round here like facing life's little problems with a smile, and prefer to die laughing. Our tale begins, as do so many, with a chance reunion.

Exit GEORGE.

HUDI: Micky.

MICKY: Hudi. How you keeping?

HUDI (*coming over*): Fair to worse, mate, how's yourself? (*He sits, not waiting for a reply.*) And how's the little woman?

RACHEL: Well, I'm just fine, Hudi. What you doing with yourself?

HUDI: Well, I'm in haulage, i'n I. Driving a van.

RACHEL: Oh, how exciting. I always dreamed of meeting someone in road haulage. Such an air of romance and mystery.

HUDI *feints punching* RACHEL *jollily.*

MICKY: Who's the other one for, Hudi?

HUDI: Meeting my friend, i'n I.

MICKY: Oh.

HUDI: Yuh. (*He sips his drink.*) Well, Micky, and how's life in a declining industry?

MICKY: I dunno, Hudi. How is it?

GEORGE *interrupts. The rest hold.*

GEORGE: 'Scuse me. An explanatory point. Neill, an ex-docker, right? Took his severance money, right? And, of course, the industry contracting, took his job with him, right? An activity viewed by our more militant brethren as not many notches up from child molesting. Just an explanatory point.

HUDI: Well, I got out when the going was good, di'n I? West London my patch. Heathrow.

Pause.

Look, mate. We all know what's

happened. Dockers got conned, di'n they. Sold their heritage for a ha'porth of security. Devlin, all that.

MICKY: All right. Go on.

GEORGE *comes in again. The rest hold.*

GEORGE: Sorry. 'Scuse me again. Another explanatory point. Devlin. His Lordship's report on the Docks, 1965. Ending The Frightful And Inhumane Casual Employment System. The Dreaded Twice-Daily Call. Grown Men Fighting For Work On The Stones. Having to bribe the gaffer for half a day's work. All that. Right?

HUDI: I mean, lovely. Dancing in the streets. Only thing, the docker wakes up one fine a.m., finds he i'n't a free agent no more. Shiftwork. Timekeeping. 'Stead of dockers deciding how they'll do a job, you got blokes with stopwatches and clipboards. And where's the famed and noted freedom of the river, then?

Slight pause.

I mean, don't get me wrong. I even voted for it. Progress. Gotta be. But, as it happens, I personally did not fancy getting caught 'twixt Devlin and the deep blue, so I has it away on me toes, and runs me own life.

Slight pause.

Play the system. Get what's going. No-one else'll do it for you.

MICKY: Know your trouble, Hudi? You're just a bleeding cowboy.

HUDI: Well, how's life on the reservation? Chief Sitting Duck?

Enter LINDA; *she looks around.*

Ah, there she is. Helen of Troy.

RACHEL: Eh?

HUDI: The face that sunk a thousand ships.

LINDA *turns, notices them. They all hold.*

GEORGE: Third explanatory point. Linda Barratt. Neill's intended. Nice girl. But dumb. So dumb, she thought

Neill was a nice bloke.

LINDA (*coming over*): Oh, there y'are. (*To* RACHEL:) Oh, hallo, Rache.

RACHEL (*in surprise and alarm*): Linda?

HUDI: Eh, you two aquainted?

RACHEL: Linda works with me at Morris's.

HUDI (*to* LINDA): You want to watch her, darling. A Trotskyist agitator.

LINDA: 'Know. She's trying to get us all in the union.

HUDI: Well, keeps her fingers busy, don' it.

RACHEL: Hey, Linda, don't want to pry, but are you in some class of relationship or liaison with this character?

LINDA (*sipping her drink*): Yuh. 'Am. Anything wrong?

RACHEL: Oh, no, nothing. Just – (*She is interrupted by a* VOICE *from off.*)

VOICE: 'S there a Mr Neill in the bar?

HUDI (*stands*): Yuh. That's me.

VOICE: Telephone.

HUDI: Who is it?

VOICE: Hold on.

Pause.

He says, 'Do us a favour'.

HUDI: Oh, it's him. Coming! 'Scuse I.

Exit HUDI. *Pause.*

RACHEL: Of course, the other good reason for Hudi leaving the dock, now, things how they are, is the reduced opportunities for tea-leafing on our hitherto accustomed scale.

MICKY: They always said, Hudi used to go in the dock looking like a seven-stone weakling, come out looking like Robert Morley.

RACHEL: Did they indeed.

Pause.

Well, Linda, just see you don't get influenced. I set myself a target, one

hundred per cent closed shop by summer, and I don't want no Annie Oakleys on my patch.

LINDA: No.

Re-enter HUDI.

MICKY: Well? Anything interesting?

HUDI: Oh, no, just a bit of business. Um, Rache –

ANNA *has entered.* HUDI, *seeing her*:

Bloody hell.

They all hold.

GEORGE: And, finally, Anna Lawrence. First year of a Social Science course at Brunel University. First day she's there, she joins Debating Soc, the Bridge Club, the Change-ringing Association, the Hockey Team and a sinister group called Workers Vanguard. So she's down here, forging links.

Slight pause.

Revolting student. Know the thing I mean?

ANNA: 'Scuse me.

HUDI: Yuh?

ANNA: I wonder if you'd like to buy a paper.

HUDI: No thanks, love, I'm a Baptist.

ANNA: No, it's a socialist paper. Fight the Tories.

HUDI: No thanks, love, I'm a Conservative Baptist.

LINDA: Hudi.

Slight pause.

MICKY: Let's have a look then.

ANNA *hands over two papers, which* MICKY *and* HUDI *start flipping through. Pause.* ANNA *glances at her watch.*

RACHEL: You in a hurry?

ANNA: Oh, no, it's just that I really ought to sell another five before closing time. You see, I've come last but one in our selling group three weeks running, and if I don't up my sales I'll be liable to compulsory self-criticism.

RACHEL: Fate worse than death.

ANNA: Indeed.

Pause.

RACHEL (*to fill the silence*): I'm Rachel.

ANNA: Oh, I'm Anna.

RACHEL: And this is Micky and this is Linda and this is Hudi.

ANNA: Hudi.

RACHEL: As in Yehudi.

ANNA: Oh, yuh.

RACHEL: Get it?

ANNA: No.

MICKY (*looking up*): Yehudi.

ANNA: Menuhin.

MICKY: Spot on.

ANNA: He plays the violin?

MICKY: No, love, but he's always on the fiddle.

ANNA: Oh, I see.

HUDI: Hey, are you the bleeding IRA?

ANNA: I'm sorry?

HUDI: What's all this about the sodding IRA?

ANNA: Oh, is that the piece on Bloody Sun-

HUDI: All this crap about the vanguard of the anti-imperialist struggle?

ANNA: Well, it's, you see, we think –

HUDI: 'Workers in Britain must stand together with the Irish Freedom Fighters in their struggle for –'

ANNA: Well, it's the unity of the –

HUDI: Look, sweetheart, I got a cousin in the military got his imperialist arm shot off by one of your –

ANNA: But it's not the . . . I mean, it's the officers, not the common, I mean, ordinary –

HUDI: Common? Common what?

ANNA: I . . .

Pause.

MICKY: Look, love, I'll take one.

ANNA: Oh, thanks.

LINDA: I'll have one too please.

HUDI *looks at* LINDA.

MICKY: How much?

ANNA: Well, they're five new pence each, but if you wanted to give a bit extra, for the Smash Internment Fund . . .

MICKY: Two bob for two, OK?

ANNA (*takes the money*): Thanks, very much. (*Not sure how to leave:*) Um – Right. See you. (*Exit.*)

HUDI *has a good laugh.*

MICKY: Cowboy.

HUDI: Well, it makes you sick, don' it. Coming in here, selling the revolution with an accent you could shave your face with –

LINDA: I thought she was nice.

HUDI: Yuh, well, I don't know why you bought one.

LINDA: Why not?

HUDI: I mean, there's not much point in you buying a sodding newspaper.

LINDA: Why not?

HUDI: Seeing as how your literary limit is round about 'The cat sat on the mat.'

RACHEL: Hudi, shut your face.

HUDI: Eh?

RACHEL: You heard.

Pause. RACHEL *stands.*

Right. Time to go time. Micky?

MICKY (*stands*): Right.

HUDI: Um, Rache –

RACHEL: Yuh?

HUDI: What kind of thing does your firm make?

Pause.

RACHEL: Why ask?

Pause.

HUDI: Why not?

GEORGE (*appearing*): Why Not Indeed.

Scene Three

Music, and into the Rag Trade Rag. During the song, the set is changed to the pressing room of a small garment factory. Two big ironing boards, at which LINDA *and* RACHEL *work. A rail of pressed garments at one side, and a skip of unpressed clothes at the other.*

Rag Trade Rag

RACHEL/LINDA:
From Whitechapel north up Brick Lane
From Aldgate out East to Mile End
The sight you'll observe is the same
It's the garment trade setting the trend
With infinite patience and care
We are fashioning what you will wear
For the East Ender's trade is
For Gents and for Ladies
We're doing the Rag Trade Rag

The cash till is ringing
Machinists are singing
We're doing the Rag Trade Rag

The music goes on under the following dialogue. Enter MORRIS, *passing across the stage.*

MORRIS: Morning, girls.

LINDA: Morning, Mr Morris.

He is nearly out when RACHEL *catches up with him.*

RACHEL: Hey, Mr Morris, I want to talk to you.

MORRIS: Not now, Rachel, there's a love. Busy morning. VIP visiting. All our futures.

RACHEL: Yuh, well, it's all our futures I want to talk about.

MORRIS: After dinner, Rachel, there's a love.

    RACHEL *goes back to her board as* MORRIS *sings:*

It's a matter of us against them
Keep your cloth in accord with your coat
Your competitor's raising his hem
And he's cutting his cloth and your throat
For you it's a change in the style
For me it's the inch that's a mile
You daren't make a bungle
The East is a jungle
You're doing the Rag Trade Rag

Competition is savage
You're living on cabbage
You're doing the Rag Trade Rag

Exit MORRIS. *The music goes on.*

RACHEL: Jammy bastard.

LINDA: What you want to see him for?

RACHEL (*holds up the denim skirt she's ironing*): This stuff. I want handling money.

LINDA: Eh?

RACHEL *lifts up the cotton skirt from* LINDA's *board to demonstrate the difference.*

RACHEL: Denim. Heavier. Rougher. More difficult to handle. Right? So we get paid for it. I'm going for tuppence a piece.

LINDA: He won't like that.

RACHEL: I'm not asking him to like it.

A bell rings.

That'll be his bleeding VIP.

MORRIS *passes across the stage, noticing* RACHEL's *scowl, gestures to them both to smile, and goes off.*

And he wants us looking happy. I think I'lll make it a tanner.

RACHEL/LINDA:
So ladies and gents don't you fret
At the prices you pay for your clothes
We're reminding you lest you forget
Someone'e sweating to keep you in vogue
When you're matching your bottom and
               top
Just remember who got it sewn up
And be sure, haute couture tends
To lose its allure when
You're doing the Rag Trade Rag.

The music ends, but a loud hum, however, continues through the scene. Enter MORRIS *with* MISS JONES, *a buyer from a fashionable boutique.*

MORRIS: And this is the pressing department.

MISS JONES: Oh, yuh?

MORRIS: And these, in fact, are my pressers.

MISS JONES: Hi.

LINDA: Hi.

RACHEL: Good morning.

MORRIS: This is Miss Jones, girls, Miss Petra Jones of Lilies of the Field.

RACHEL: Lilies of the what?

MORRIS: Field, Rachel. It's a Bibilical reference. As in, they sow not, neither do they reap.

MISS JONES *is looking through the clothes on the rail.*

RACHEL: Well, that sets them apart from your machinists, don't it? They're sewing all the hours God sends.

MORRIS (*laughs, then*): Lilies of the Field, Rachel dear. Of King's Road. As in, Chelsea. Miss Jones is a buyer. As in money.

MISS JONES (*picking out a denim skirt*): This it then?

MORRIS: That is indeed it.

MISS JONES: Yuh. Any chance of seeing it on?

MORRIS: Um, is the particular garment S, M or L?

MISS JONES (*looking*): S.

MORRIS (*a glance at* RACHEL): Thank the good lord for that. (*He takes the skirt and hands it to* LINDA.) Linda would you mind slipping this on?

LINDA: What, here?

MORRIS: No, lover, in the Ladies'.

LINDA *goes out with the skirt.*
RACHEL *is ironing away.*

RACHEL: You might like a glance at the Ladies', Miss Jones.

MORRIS: Rachel, my sweet –

RACHEL: You might also like to note that the rail you took the particular garment from is blocking the ventilator. Hence the sub-tropical atmosphere.

MORRIS: I should explain, Miss Jones, that Rachel is our Resident Red.

Someone foolishly gave her A Child's Guide to Marxism for Christmas, and I'm sincerely hoping that next year it'll be something normal like nylons.

MISS JONES: Oh, yuh. Hey, talking of nylons –

MORRIS: Yes?

MISS JONES: D'you hear about Courtaulds.

MORRIS: No I did not hear about Courtaulds.

MISS JONES: Thought the bottom was going to fall out of trousers, di'n't they. So to speak. So they thought they was being bloody clever, kept the tights line going, while everyone else moving on. Course, the silly bleeders got landed. Bloody funny, eh?

MORRIS: Yes. Bloody funny.

Re-enter LINDA *in the skirt.*

Ah. Pretty as a picture.

MISS JONES (*looking for the light source*): Um –

MORRIS: Yes, Linda, why not come into the light.

The three go downstage, quite a way from RACHEL.

MISS JONES *looking*: Yuh. Very nice. What's the touch?

MORRIS: Perhaps we could discuss that in my office.

MISS JONES: I mean, you're manu-facturing yourself. Not outwork.

MORRIS: Oh, no. It's my own material you see.

MISS JONES (*feeling the skirt*): Bloody good stuff. Twelve ounce, i'n it? Where you get it?

MORRIS: Well, shall we say – thank you, Linda –

LINDA *is going but she overhears*:

I have a source of supply. Hence the attractive nature of the touch.

MISS JONES: Oh. 'See. Well.

MORRIS *turns back to* LINDA; LINDA *goes back to her board.*

MORRIS: If you could, perhaps, step through –

MISS JONES: Yuh. Ta.

MORRIS *and* MISS JONES *go out.*

LINDA: Hey, Rache –

RACHEL: Bloody woman.

LINDA: Um, Rache –

RACHEL: And you ought to get ten quid for modelling and all. What?

LINDA: Did you hear what Morris said?

RACHEL: No. What?

Semi-blackout and the hum stops.

LINDA: What's that?

RACHEL (*immediately stopping work*): Power cut. Well, that's it for four hours. May as well go and tell the girls to knock off.

Enter MORRIS.

MORRIS: What's going on? Why've the machines stopped?

RACHEL: It's a power cut, Mr Morris. As in, miners' strike.

MORRIS: Oh. Yes. The lights have gone.

RACHEL (*walking out*): Which you'd have noticed if your office wasn't the only room in the building with reasonable access to a window.

MORRIS: Hey, where are you going?

RACHEL: Tell the girls to knock off.

MORRIS: Knock off? They can do hand-work, can't they?

RACHEL: With no heating? In mid-winter?

MORRIS: Rachel, I don't understand you. One minute it's sub-tropical, next minute you're all freezing to death. (RACHEL *looks at* MORRIS *and goes. To* LINDA:) And you can get that skirt off before you spill something on it. (*He marches out.* LINDA *gives a V-sign to his departure. She tidies her board for a moment. Re-enter* RACHEL.)

RACHEL: Right, then. 'Bout what Morris said. Shoot.

LINDA: Well –

They are interrupted by the music of the Rag Trade Rag, which covers the change.

Scene Four

Another pub. Two tables, each with two chairs, downstage and either side of a bar billiards table, on which RACHEL and NICKY are playing. Enter GEORGE.

GEORGE: February the 10th, 1972. State of Emergency. Britain on the Brink. Miners Holding the Country to Ransom. All that while, in a back-street bar-room, the plot, with the atmosphere, is thickening.

Exit GEORGE. RACHEL and MICKEY talk as they play:

RACHEL: Well?

MICKY: Problem is, what you do about it.

RACHEL: There's people on ten, eleven quid in there, Micky –

MICKY: Yuh, I know. It's what you do about it.

HUDI *and* LINDA *have entered.* HUDI *is carrying a carton.*

HUDI: Good evening, one and each.

He plonks the carton on the edge of the billiard table.

MICKY: Hallo, mate. What's that then?

HUDI: Candles.

MICKY: Eh?

HUDI: As in, highly short supply. Can I interest you in a discount order?

MICKY: Blimey. How many you got there?

HUDI: Well, there's a dozen a pack, and twenty packs, so work it out.

MICKY: Where d'you get them?

HUDI: Shall we say, they fell off the back of an altar.

MICKY: I'll think about it.

HUDI *takes the carton to one of the tables, puts it down. As he does so:*

HUDI: Fancy doubles?

RACHEL *looks at* MICKY.

MICKY: If you like.

HUDI (*coming back over*): Great. So, what's the bother?

MICKY: Bother?

HUDI (*quoting* MICKY): 'I know. It's what you do about it'.

MICKY: Oh, yuh. Rachel reckons Morris has got a supply of bent fabric.

HUDI (*chalking his cue*): Oh, yuh. Linda said. So?

RACHEL: So if he's getting cheap gear, he's ripping us off even more than usual.

HUDI: So what d'you plan doing about it?

RACHEL: Stopping him.

HUDI: How?

RACHEL: How d'you usually stop people receiving stolen goods.

Pause. HUDI *gives* LINDA *a pound note.*

HUDI: Go and get them in, love.

RACHEL: Get them in yourself, Hudi.

HUDI: Go and get them in love.

LINDA *goes.*

(*Preparing to shoot:*) Let's get this clear. You're proposing shopping your employer –

RACHEL: Well, I'm not saying –

HUDI: To the filth. Right?

RACHEL: Hudi, you ever heard of exploitation. It's a technical term for bosses paying workers less than the value they produce. And if bosses get their raw materials for bugger all, then they're exploiting their workers even more.

HUDI: Well, Rache, my sweet –

RACHEL: I'm not your sweet.

LINDA *comes back with the drinks during:*

HUDI: Can I make a suggestion? Now, you're a shop steward, right? Now, if I was you, I'd go along to Mr Morris and say, look here, Morry, a little bird's whispering as how this gear we're working isn't totally kosher. And he says Oh my gawd discovered. And you says Dead Right you is Morry. And he falls to his knees and says Oh Please Dear Rachel do not shop me to the filth I will do anything just name it and it's yours. And you says, nonchalant, like, you says, Well Morry there is one thing now you mention it how about a raise all round and we can call it quits. (*He plays a shot.*) That's what I'd do.

RACHEL: That's blackmail.

HUDI: Well spotted.

RACHEL: Look. Do you know why the Rag Trade is so badly organised? 'Cos there's hundreds of little shops doing precisely that kind of undercover wheeling and dealing and that's why pay is sometimes quite good but conditions are dire and –

HUDI: Suit yourself. It's your exploited sisters and broth-

MICKY *stops him, he's seen someone approaching. The someone enters, a* MINER. *He has a collecting tin and a card.*

MINER (*showing his card*): Good evening, brothers and sisters. Official National Union of Mineworkers collection. Support the miners' strike.

They all put money in with their lines:

MICKY: Yuh, sure.

RACHEL: Yuh, 'course.

HUDI: Here y'are, mate.

LINDA: Good luck.

MINER: Thank you, brothers and sisters.

Exit MINER. *Straight on:*

RACHEL: Micky, what you think?

MICKY: I think, I mean, I think –

RACHEL: Spit it out, Micky.

MICKY: You can't shop him, Rache.

RACHEL: Oh, see. Linda?

HUDI: She agrees with me.

LINDA: I don't agree with you.

HUDI (*ignoring her, waving towards where the* MINER *went out*): According to my Daily Express, the miners are blackmailing the nation.

Pause.

RACHEL: Hudi, the way the miners is holding the country to ransom is by involving the whole movement in what they're doing. You get railmen not crossing pickets. Dockers blacking coal. Engineers in Birmingham helping to stop coke moving. Right? Good. Now, are you suggesting that that's the same as me –

HUDI (*interrupting*): All right. Point taken. Class struggle. Collective action. Clenched fists on the barricades. My heart is duly warmed.

Slight pause. LINDA *is about to play her shot.*

Hey, Lind, you agree with Rache. You do the job. Here's two p, you go phone Old Bill.

LINDA: Eh?

HUDI: Go on.

LINDA *plays her shot. Disaster.*

Oh, blimey. You stupid cow.

LINDA, *upset, goes to the table with the carton on it and sits.*

RACHEL: Hudi, you really are a grade A bastard, aren't you?

HUDI: Rachel, you may well be right, but are you proposing squealing on whoever's running gear into your shop?

Slight pause.

Are you?

RACHEL (*furious*): NO.

She goes and sits with LINDA. MICKY, *giving a half-shrug to* HUDI, *goes and joins them.* HUDI *continues to play by himself. Slight pause.*

MICKY: Rache, I think you've –

RACHEL: Change the subject.

MICKY: 'K.

Pause.

What was that 'bout Birmingham engineers, you was saying?

RACHEL: Oh, there's a coke depot, place called Saltley. Miners' pickets trying to get the car firms out, to close it.

MICKY: Yuh? You know, we ought to think 'bout that.

RACHEL: What?

MICKY: That kind of picketing. You know, for our little problem down here.

LINDA: What problem's that?

MICKY: Well –

HUDI (*brightly, coming over to them*): I shall explain.

RACHEL *stands, walking out.*

Rachel? You off?

RACHEL (*acidly*): I'm going to the little woman's room. (*Exit.*)

HUDI: Ah, well, you can't win 'em all. Now – (*Taking* LINDA's *hand*) – with the aid of my lovely assistant . . .

Slight pause. He kisses her hand. LINDA *half shrugs, stands.* HUDI *leads her over to the other table, taking a chair which he puts halfway between the two. He goes back to the table with the carton on it, and empties the carton on to the empty chair, dropping the now empty carton on the floor.*

Right, Micky. Your little problem. Explanation of. Watch closely.

He picks up as many candles as he can hold and takes them to LINDA, *clambering over the centre chair. He gives the packs to* LINDA *and walks back, round the chair to the other table again. Then he gestures to* LINDA *to do the same in reverse. She comes to him, climbing over the chair, hands the packs of candles to him.*

Right.

He drops the packs on the chair. Takes LINDA *back to where she was. As he does so:*

Linda was a factory abroad. I was a factory at home.

Leaving LINDA, *he goes to the centre chair.*

This is the docks. Slow, wasteful and expensive.

He goes back to the chair with the candles.

Eureka.

He sweeps the packs of candles into the carton, and picks it up.

Quick. Efficient. Cheap. Containers.

He throws the carton, over the chair in the middle, to LINDA, *who catches it.* HUDI *turns to* MICKY.

Sorry, mate. Progress.

He takes a sip of his pint. RACHEL *re-enters.* HUDI *puts down his glass, turns back to* LINDA. *At that moment,* LINDA *throws the carton back, to frighten* HUDI. RACHEL, *who's reached the centre chair, catches it before it reaches* HUDI.

RACHEL: They got a telly in the lounge. On News at Ten. 10,000 engineers came out in Brum. They just closed Saltley. (*She drops the carton on to the centre chair.*) That's progress.

Music.

Scene Five

At once, into the song. During it MICKY *sets up a ship's hold. He is piling boxes onto a trolley.*

Technology

SONG:
It is certainly and absolutely true
That technology is good for me and you
Its purpose is to build a better land
As you can see
Technology
For you and me

It is actually and factually so
That life improves with everything we
know
The whole world will be fabulously grand
As you can see

Technology
For you and me

It's demonstrably and definitely the case
We must forge ahead to keep us in the
race
There's just one problem, we are sad to
say
There's some people who are getting in
the way

The problem is, you're grossly over-
manned
Why can't you see
Technology
For you and me

Enter GEORGE.

GEORGE: Right. A little further plot. The end of Feb, 1972. The miners win. That leaves the dockers' little problem. Twenty-ton containers, don't need dockers. They don't mind it, when it's full containers, factory to factory. But they do mind it, very much, when it's what they call cowboy groupage depots, packing loads from lots of different factories, just outside dockland, using non-dock labour, paying non-dock rates. That does expand their nostrils. More than somewhat.

MICKY (*stops work, looks up, addresses the audience*): The courts done nothing, said the stewards. Taken 18 cases to the courts, lost 17. We take it in our own hands, said the stewards. Black the depots, don't we. (*He resumes his work.*)

GEORGE: And then it's March. And the Liverpool dockers do indeed black the depots. And come smack up against the newly set up National Industrial Relations Court, known none-too-affectionately as the Nirc, which blames the union, the T&G, and fines 'em fifty grand. Jack Jones coughs up. But that don't stop the blacking spreading. Down to London. Place called Chobham Farm.

MICKY: You know, the stewards said, that Chobham Farm is owned by Cunard and Tom Wallis. Dock employers. Stole our jobs, the stewards said: We're going to steal 'em back.

GEORGE: And then it's June. And Jack Jones appeals against the fine. Success-

fully. So the fine is quashed. But, if
the T&G ain't responsible, who is?
Dead right. The stewards. Blacking
goes on, stewards going to get it in the
neck. You know a steward got a ready
fifty grand?

Exit GEORGE. *Pause.*

MICKY: A whole new ball game. Now
can fine us, even jail us. Now the
stakes are really high.

Slight pause.

We said.

Slight pause.

Not only up against employers. Up
against the State.

Enter DON, *a stevedore.* MICKY *turns
to him. Brightly:*

Morning, Donny.

Scene Six

The Pickets' Song starts. MICKY *and
DON are among the singers. A pickets'
banner is set up:* ROYAL GROUP OF
DOCKS SHOP STEWARDS'
COMMITTEE ARISE YE WORKERS.

Pickets' Song

SONG:
It started with the pickets
Going on at Chobham Farm
The owners of the depots
Viewed the pickets with alarm
The dockers said, It's dockwork
And the depots said, It's ours
So the dockers stopped the lorries
And the trucks and vans and cars
The depots said: This is an act of war
And workers took the dockers off to law

We should be in
You should keep out
We should be in, keep out
Better turn back
Or you'll be black
We should be in, keep out

And the law ground into motion and
Injunctions they were sought
And fellow workers took the dockers
To the bosses' court
Judge Donaldson he ordered that

Three lads should go to jail
So down we went to Chobham Farm
We knew we mustn't fail
And told them, If you break that human
wall
There won't be jails enough to hold us all

One in the dock
All out in the docks
One in the dock, all out
Botany Bay's
Not far away
One in the dock, all out

The Ruling Class was terrified
The law was brought to book
They dredged up a solicitor
To get them off the hook
The Appeal Court told Judge Donaldson
That there was not a case
They didn't jail the dockers, so
They didn't lose their face
They hoped the deadly peril it had gone
The dockers said, The picketing goes on

The picket forms. It includes MICKY
and DON.

We should be in
You should keep out
We should be in, keep out
This is our work
Bugger the Nirc
We should be in, keep out

MICKY: And, as it happens, we got an
agreement with Chobham Farm. And
moved on to another cowboy depot,
Midland Cold Storage, Hackney
Marshes.

DON: Here's one.

MICKY: Right.

By some device, a lorry drives on.
MICKY *goes and stops it.*

Morning, brother. Docks picket. The
work done in this depot is traditional
dock work and –

The driver looks down from his cab.
It's HUDI.

HUDI: Hello, Micky.

MICKY: Oh, blimey. Hudi.

HUDI: What's going on here, then?
Royals Annual Outing, is it? Visiting
the stately coldstores of England?

MICKY: Hudi. Turnaround.

HUDI: Well, can't stop here chatting. Got a living to make, a'n I. See you, Mick.

MICKY: Hudi, bugger off, for God's sake.

HUDI: So if you could request your thick red line to part and let me through . . .

DON *comes over*.

Ah, here's your mate. King Kong.

MICKY *gratefully withdraws*.

DON: Morning, brother.

HUDI: Morning, brother.

DON: You know what's going on here?

HUDI: Well, seems to me as how a gang of dockers is stopping me carrying out my legitimate business. That's how it looks this end.

DON: All right. If that's the score. Explain what's happening. You cross that line –

HUDI: Like I'm just about to –

DON: And your number goes down on what we call the Cherry Blossom list –

HUDI: Oh, blacking, yes, highly droll –

DON: Yuh, i'n it, and then, by the miracle of telephonics, it goes all round the country, does your number, and you don't get in no port, nowhere, from here to Lerwick.

HUDI: Oh, I see. A kind of – Docks' Protection Racket.

Pause.

You are threatening me.

Pause.

Well, what a pleasant chat, and now –

DON (*interrupts*): We've had a lot of co-op, other drivers. One bloke, just got this haulage job, been out of work six months, he knew he'd get the push, but he didn't cross the line.

HUDI: The silly bugger.

Pause.

DON: Well, that's the score, brother. Your decision. (*He walks away.*)

HUDI (*calls*): Hey, brother?

DON (*calls back*): Yes, brother?

HUDI: Question.

DON (*comes back over*): Yuh?

HUDI: You ever thought of living in the Twentieth Century?

DON: Go on.

HUDI: I mean, had you ever thought that p'raps some people had more important things to do than worrying 'bout protecting a gang of Mick yobboes like you, from having to work for a living? (*Pause. He takes a card from his pocket.*) Know what that is? It's a driving licence. Obtainable from the Ministry of Transport. Why not get one, eh? Grow up.

DON (*furious*): You just remember one thing, pal, you can't drive nothing with one arm. And I mean that. Now you just turn that van around, and get your arse right out of here.

Slight pause. For the first time, HUDI *looks frightened.*

And, if I was you, pal, I wouldn't show my face round here for quite a while. I really wouldn't, brother.

Suddenly, HUDI *drives out. Pause.* DON, *recovering from his anger, turns to the others, and says, as a little joke, with a slight shrug:*

We have vays of stopping you valk.

And the reprise of the Picket's Song covers the change:

SONG:
We should be in
You should keep out
We should be in, keep out
This is our work
Bugger the Nirc
We should be in, keep out.

Scene Seven

Bare stage. HUDI's *place.* HUDI *enters, followed by* LINDA. HUDI *clumsily carrying a too-full, open suitcase. He drops it on the floor, tries to shut it, as:*

LINDA: Where you going, Hudi?

HUDI: North.

LINDA: Where north?

HUDI: Dunno.

LINDA: Why you going?

HUDI: None of your business.

LINDA: 'Tis my business. Why you going?

HUDI (*looks up from his task*): Look, darling. Some aggravation, right? No need to bother your pretty little head, and all. OK? (*He returns to trying to shut the case.*)

LINDA: No, not OK.

HUDI: What?

LINDA: Not OK. I want to know.

HUDI (*looks up*): *What?*

LINDA: I want to know why and where you're going. And for how long. 'S my right.

HUDI: Look, sunshine. You don't have no rights. You're only my bleeding wife in common law, with the accent on the former. (*He shuts the case, stands.*) Right.

LINDA: Where. Why. How long?

HUDI: OK, darling. (*He takes a box of matches from his pocket, gives them to LINDA.*) Here you are.

LINDA: What's them for.

HUDI: So you can burn your bra and all. (*He picks up the case, makes to go.*)

LINDA: Hudi, you bugger off without telling me where and why, and that's it.

HUDI *puts down the case.*

Mean it. Chuck you in.

HUDI (*furious, grabs* LINDA's *wrists*): Look, you say that once more, and I land you one, my love, I had it up to here, can't take it no more.

Pause.

LINDA (*deliberately*): Hudi. You bugger off, and that's it.

Pause.

Well, go on. Do as you said. Land one on my pretty little head.

Further verse of the Picket's Song, during which the next scene is set up.

SONG:
And then it was the others
Kicking back against the knocks
The lorry drivers picketed
The depots and the docks
They said, you don't expect us to
Give in without a fuss
We're not prepared to let the dockers
Walk all over us
With glee, the press reported their alarm
At being told, you can't drive with one arm

Should you be in
Should we keep out
Should you be in, us out?
You want a fight
Well, that's all right
If it's you in, us out.

Scene Eight

LINDA *and* WPC RAYNOR *are sitting at a table on one side. Enter* GEORGE *on the other. It's a Police Station.*

GEORGE: Well, hallo once more. Things moved on, since we last met. Great events stirring. But, as the back of any matchbox reminds us, even in times of grave crises, life goes on. The wheels of history may well be revolving at 78 rpm, but still, behind the banners and the barricades, you find the little human tragedies. Like Linda's.

GEORGE *goes to the table.* WPC RAYNOR *stands.*

GEORGE: Well now, Linda. Are we being a good girl, and co-operating with WPC Raynor?

LINDA: What 'm I in here for.

GEORGE: You're in here for your own protection, my flower. Can't have you wandering round London at four in the morning in your state of health. (*He picks up* LINDA's *bruised wrist.*) I mean, someone has been doing you over, my sweet, and we'd be falling down on our duty if we didn't do something about it.

LINDA: 'Thought s'posed to be a free country.

GEORGE: Oh, Linda, what a romantic you are. WPC, a word in your shell-like.

GEORGE *moves a few paces away, followed by* RAYNOR. LINDA *V-signs their departure.*

GEORGE: Well?

RAYNOR: Well, I dunno, Sarge. I mean, we can't keep her, can we? *She* hasn't done anything wrong.

GEORGE: A'n't she?

RAYNOR: Well, no, Sarge. And the bloke who did her over, her bloke, he's gone off, and she won't say where, and we can hardly force her.

GEORGE: Oh, her bloke, was it?

RAYNOR: That's right. Proper old job, too. Bruises all over her face and wrists. And God knows where else.

GEORGE: Yuh. Wrists. Odd.

RAYNOR: Oh, no, Sarge, what he'll have done is grabbed her round the –

GEORGE: No, I mean odd that she's wearing a watch on each one.

Pause.

RAYNOR: Beg pardon?

GEORGE: She's wearing two wrist-watches. Well, I say two. No doubt there's another half dozen going up each arm. So why don't you give the lady a polite going over, while I secure a W to do her bloke's place.

RAYNOR: I'm sorry, Sarge?

GEORGE: Look, petal, words of one. She's turned him over, a'n't she?

RAYNOR: Has she?

GEORGE: Look, he gives her a hiding. Way blue yonders. His gaff's oozing schmutter, right? So she lifts what she can carry, and disappears into the night. So we go and have a look for the remainder.

RAYNOR: Oh, I see.

GEORGE: Marvellous. So go and do her over, tulip. Thoroughly. Try and repress your noted squeam.

RAYNOR: Right.

RAYNOR *goes back to* LINDA. GEORGE *out front:*

GEORGE: Graduate. Honours. London School of Economics. They don't live in the real world. (*Exit.*)

RAYNOR: OK, Linda. Hands on head.

LINDA: What's this? Al Capone?

RAYNOR: Just do as you're told.

LINDA *shrugs, puts her hands on her head.* RAYNOR *pulls up her sleeves. Indeed, a couple of watches on each arm.*

Oh Linda.

LINDA *puts her arms down.* RAYNOR *picks up* LINDA's *handbag, empties it on the table. Various other goodies come to light.*

Oh dear. Well, best complete the tally, eh? Strip off.

LINDA: You what.

RAYNOR: You heard. I'm 'fraid it's what we call a comprehensive.

LINDA (*for form*): 'Want to see my –

RAYNOR: Leave it out, love.

LINDA *slowly stands as* GEORGE *re-enters to them.*

GEORGE: Excuse me, ladies.

LINDA *sits.*

Just for your information, WPC, 'fore you start on madam, guess what them harvests have done.

RAYNOR: Which loons, Sarge?

GEORGE: They of the grey ringlets, darling. They of the red silk, and, in happier days, the little black cap.

RAYNOR: So what they done, Sarge?

GEORGE: They only jailed five bleeding dockers, a'n't they? I mean, not just threatened to. Actually gone and done it.

RAYNOR: Blimey.

GEORGE: Blimey is the *mot juste*, my dear old dahlia. Well, just thought I'd let you know. Now I'll go and get that W. (*He makes to go, then turns and declaims at the bemused* WPC RAYNOR:) And I bet that judge is a bleeding graduate and all.

Further chorus of the Picket's Song as the scene changes.

SONG:
Five are inside
Why aren't you out
Five are inside, all out
This is their law
This is our war
Five are inside, come out.

Scene Nine

Table, behind, two chairs. RACHEL *stands at the table. This is a meeting at the garment factory. The interruptions come over the mikes from invisible* WORKERS: ONE *and* TWO *are women,* THREE *is a man.*

RACHEL: All right, brothers and sisters, can we have some order.

Slight pause.

Right, meeting today, I called, to discuss whether or not we want to take action in support of the dockers.

Pause.

The five dockers who're in jail. And we got here, Brother Don Hall, from the Royals, who's going to introduce the, introduce the meeting. Brother Hall.

Enter DON. *He goes to the table.* RACHEL *sits and lights a cigarette as he begins to speak.*

DON: Ta. Brothers and sisters, first, I'd like to thank you for inviting me here –

WORKER ONE: We didn't!

DON: – thank your shop steward for inviting me here. Now, what I want to do is, correct one or two things that's being said about us, in the press and so on, 'cos I think a lot of people's getting the wrong impression 'bout what's

been actually happening.

WORKER TWO (*ambiguously*): Hear hear.

Slight pause.

DON: Thank you. For one thing, we got our Prime Minister, Ted the Teeth – (*Slight pause*) – going on the telly and calling Midland Cold Store, and I quote, 'a pathetic little firm being driven into bankruptcy.' And pathetic's right and all. ' Cos we done a bit of digging, and found that Midland Cold Store is owned by quote the Ulster Bank of Belfast unquote. And Ulster Bank is owned by none other than the Vestey Family. And we all know who they are.

Slight pause.

WORKER THREE: Who's they, then?

DON: Well. All right. If you don't know –

WORKER THREE: We're pig ignorant, see.

Slight pause.

DON: Well. Lord Samuel Vestey. Who inherited his first million when he was a fag at Eton, now what's he. Well, he's a livestock farmer in Australia. And a shipowner. And a stevedoring employer. And a haulage contractor. And a butcher. And now this pathetic little concern is a cowboy coldstore entrepreneur and all. Which is why we pickets it. And –

WORKER TWO: Hey, brother –

DON: Yuh?

WORKER TWO: I got a question.

DON: Yuh?

WORKER TWO: Want to know what you think 'bout the lorry drivers you turned away picketing the dock.

DON: Well, sister, we regret it, but their action will give work to our brothers on the barges and lighters and –

WORKER TWO: I should explain, my brother drives a lorry. Brother.

Slight pause.

Says, they'd mind less if the dockers

ever told them 'bout what's going on.

DON: Hey, now, that's –

WORKER ONE: And what about the workers at Chobham Farm, you got your jobs, what 'bout them?

DON: They're fine, sweetheart. Particularly as how, since registered men moved in to do the stuffing and stripping, they're all on dock rates of pay.

WORKER THREE: Anyone still there.

DON: They're all still there, mate. That's another Tory lie. No-one was made redundant. That was in our agreement and all.

WORKER TWO: Hey brother?

DON: Yuh?

WORKER TWO: I'm very impressed.

DON: That's nice.

WORKER TWO: But I do wonder whether, sooner or later, you're going to have to learn to live with progress.

Slight pause.

DON: Progress, eh? Right. Let me ask a question. Progress for whom. Well, obviously not us, but leave that out. What about the consumer. Well. The docks so expensive, wasteful. Well. Ten times less people needed for containers. Well. Where's the saving going. Prices going down? Eh? Progress for whom. Have a guess.

Pause.

Do anything, to do us down. What you work on here?

WORKER ONE: Bugger all!

RACHEL (*smiling, with* DON): Well, lots – cotton, corduroy, denim –

DON: Right, denim. Probably comes from Hong Kong, shipped to Rotterdam, unloaded, and flown to Heathrow. And it costs more than going through London, but they're doing it so they've an excuse to close another dock. And they're going for the dockers, like they went for the miners, 'cos they know as how once they smashed us –

WORKER THREE: Hey –

DON: They smashed the whole movement, and –

WORKER THREE: Hey, I wanna ask you a question.

DON (*impatiently*): OK. What?

WORKER THREE: Simple question. What you dockers ever done for us? Why we should lose money to protect you dockers?

Pause. RACHEL *stands.*

RACHEL: I'll answer that.

WORKER THREE: I want him to tell –

RACHEL: Look, shut it, Jimmy, all right?

Slight pause. DON *sits.*

Right. We support the dockers now like we supported them in 1958, and 1949, and during the 30s, and all the way back to 19 bleeding 12.

WORKER ONE: Lest auld acquaintance be forgot –

RACHEL: Sure, sure, and I'll tell you why. 'Cos when you talk about protection, let's be clear. The dockers have fought for their protection. 'Gainst casualism. 'Gainst the fact that docking's seasonal, and –

WORKER TWO: So's the rag trade, Rachel –

RACHEL: Yuh, right, and wouldn't you prefer it if your fathers and grandfathers had fought so we weren't taken on for two months and then thrown down the road? Fought so we had guaranteed wages?

Pause.

That's what the Tories is trying to smash. 'Xactly that. Workers protecting themselves. But there's a way of stopping them doing that. By workers protecting each other. (*Slight pause.*) We might have disagreements, with the dockers. Some of us may have relatives had bother at the depots. Fine. But that's our business. Not the government's. Or the courts. Or the prisons. (*Slight pause.*) So, you vote to come out, you're not coming out for the dockers. You're coming out with them. Right?

Pause.

Right? Anyone else?

Pause.

OK, we'll have a vote. All in favour, coming out.

Pause.

Against? (*She sits.*) Meeting closed. We're coming out.

The workers leave. Pause. DON *offers* RACHEL *a cigarette. They light up.*

RACHEL: Ta.

Pause. DON *stands.*

DON: My great grandad came from County Sligo. And he became a corn porter in the Surrey. Toughest job in the port. And a killer, grain dust. Gets the lungs, eventually. But that didn't stop him fighting mechanisation in the 1880s. 'Cos they had status. I'm proud my great grandad was a bulk-grain worker. Even though he died of it. Does that make any sense?

Pause.

RACHEL: Yuh. Well. My great grandad came from St Petersburg, in the hold of a timber ship, during a pogrom in 1899. Make any sense?

DON *smiles.*

DON: Ta, Rachel.

He goes. Music.

Stick Together

RACHEL:
From the corners of the world
Here we came
West Indians and Irish
Just the same
Whence and whither we've come
We're all of us foreign scum

Stick together
to protect ourselves
Sister and brother
Stick together
to protect each other

From the corners of the world
The aliens

The Cypriots and Jews
And Asians
Micks and Dagoes and Frogs
We're all of us Yids and Wogs

Stick together, *etc*

And the **Pickets' Song** in again, big:

SONG:
'Cos split apart they'll drive a wedge
                            right through
'Cos stuck together, nothing we can't do

Five are inside
Why aren't you out
Five are inside, all out
This is class law
This is class war
Five are inside, ALL OUT.

Scene Ten

A tube train. MICKY.

MICKY: They'd gone in, the five, on the Friday. And people heard the news, went home, had a wash and a shave, and something to eat, and went down there, and stayed for days. I lasted till Tuesday night. Then I went home, had a bath, and slept for fourteen hours. Back down to Pentonville next day.

Enter a tube-sign, THE ANGEL, *behind* MICKY. *The 'train' stops, doors open,* MICKY *out. A passenger runs in to catch the train, bumps into* MICKY. *The passenger is* HUDI.

MICKY: Sorry, mate.

MICKY *passes on,* HUDI *realises.*

HUDI: Hey, Micky.

MICKY: Oh, Christ, Hudi.

Sound of tube doors closing. HUDI *turns to see,* MICKY *takes the opportunity to turn and makes to go.* HUDI *ignores the train, and goes after* MICKY. *Sound of train leaving.*

HUDI: Micky.

MICKY: Yuh? What d'you want?

HUDI: Micky.

MICKY: I said, what d'you want?

HUDI: Micky, family quarrel, wa'n't it.

MICKY: Was it?

HUDI: Micky. Brother 'gainst brother. When an outsider puts the boot in, close ranks, don't you.

MICKY: Do you?

HUDI: Lorry drivers' pickets off at once, when they went inside, weren't they?

MICKY: Were they?

HUDI: Micky, make it a bit easier, for God's sake.

MICKY: Where's Linda, Hudi? Hasn't been to work, since you buggered off.

HUDI: I don't know, do I? A'n't been home. Got back today.

Pause.

MICKY: Look, I gotta –

HUDI: Look, I didn't know they'd jail them, did I? Didn't know the stakes were that high, did I?

MICKY: No. We none of us knew that.

Pause. Slight smile

Look, mate, OK, but got to go up to Pentonville, all right?

HUDI: Up Pentonville?

MICKY: That's right.

HUDI: I wouldn't bother.

MICKY: Why not? Picket.

HUDI: I'n't no picket, Micky.

Pause. MICKY moves towards HUDI, angry.

MICKY: What d'you mean?

HUDI: Hardly much point now, is there?

MICKY: Now – ?

HUDI: They're out.

Pause.

Just come from there. They're out. You won. Look, wondered if you and Rache, care to join me, take a jaunt up West, to celebrate, know what I . . .

Pause.

Don't just stand there like a slab of haddock, Micky. Don't you see? You won.

MICKY (*suddenly*): All right. That case. You're on.

A huge drumming culminates, oddly, in a jolly little German operetta-drinking-song istrumental which covers the change.

Scene Eleven

A Bierkeller in the West End. A table, chairs. Enter HUDI, RACHEL and MICKY. The music fades, but carries on in the background.

HUDI (*to explain*): It's a Bierkeller.

RACHEL: Oh, yuh?

HUDI: You know. A Teutonic Alchouse. Deutschland Über Watneys.

RACHEL: Right.

HUDI: I'll go and get 'em in, then. Lager?

MICKY: When in Düsseldorf. Yuh. Pint.

RACHEL: And a pint for me, Hudi.

HUDI: Micky, you're going to have to do something 'bout your missus.

RACHEL: What's that?

HUDI: Oh nothing.

Exit HUDI. RACHEL and MICKY sit.

MICKY: Well?

RACHEL: Where's Linda, Micky?

MICKY: Didn't ask. I will.

Slight pause.

RACHEL: What was it again? A gang of Mick yobboes?

MICKY: What does your mum think of dockers?

Pause.

RACHEL: OK, Micky. I'll try and enjoy myself.

MICKY: Good.

RACHEL: But I can't understand why –

MICKY *stops her as* HUDI *comes back. He's empty-handed.*

HUDI: Waitress service only. But I placed the order and they'll send someone . . . (*He's embarrassed.*) Look, we could go to a pub if you –

MICKY: Hudi, it's OK. Really.

HUDI *sits.*

HUDI: Great.

Pause.

Eh, you see Ted Heath on the box?

MICKY: No.

HUDI (*imitating*): What has happened today is that the Industrial Relations Act has been completely justified and vindicated. That is why the five dockers have been released. That's not luck it's the law of the land.

MICKY *and* RACHEL *laugh.*

I still don't quite get how it happened.

MICKY: Well, what it was, the House of Lords reversed the Appeal Court's decision. So the stewards i'n't responsible, it's the union. 'Course, complete coincidence they happened to decide that while five lads were inside . . .

HUDI: Hey, I was in the pub lunchtime, heard, well, overheard, this story. Shah of Persia, see. Richest bloke in the world. Anyway, it's Christmas, and he asks his three sons what they want. And the oldest, 25, he says he wants an aeroplane. And the Shah says, OK, but he don't get him any old aeroplane, he gets him the Concorde. And the next one, he's 15, and says he wants a boat. And the Shah says, no bother, but he don't get him any old boat, he gets him the QE2. And the third song, he's seven, he says, what I really want's a cowboy outfit. And the Shah says, OK, that's cool, but he don't get him just any old cowboy outfit, he goes out and gets him Midland Cold Storage.

Amusement.

Eh, and have you heard the one about about –

But he's interrupted by the entrance of the waitress with a tray of lagers. The waitress, who is dressed in cod German costume, is ANNA.

ANNA: Sorry to be so long. Three pints of – Jesus.

HUDI: Pardon?

RACHEL: Oh, hallo.

HUDI: What?

RACHEL: Fancy meeting you here.

ANNA: Yes, it's –

HUDI: Rache, are you acquainted with –

RACHEL: It's Anna, Hudi. Who didn't sell you a copy of her newspaper.

MICKY: Oh. right. Hallo, love.

ANNA: Hallo.

Pause.

ANNA: ⎱ Look, I'd better –
HUDI: ⎰ Look, could I enquire –

ANNA: Go on.

HUDI: Just enquire, a) what you doing, and b) why you're doing it dressed as Eva Braun.

ANNA: Vacation job. They make you wear the costume. Atmosphere. (*Slight pause.*) Are you celebrating, you know, the five?

MICKY: That's right. You ought to join us.

ANNA: Well, I can't, rea-

RACHEL: Oh, come on –

ANNA: No, you see, I –

MICKY: Come on, sit down.

ANNA: So, if I did, you see, I'd lose –

HUDI: Well, bloody hell. Thought you was a bleeding revolutionary.

MICKY: Hudi.

ANNA: No, it's, you see, I need the money . . .

Pause.

Look, I really must . . . (*She tears the bill off her pad, puts it on the table and goes.*)

RACHEL: Don't you meet people in the strangest places.

HUDI: Bit embarrassing, really. I think she was embarrassed.

RACHEL: Well, how amazingly perceptive of you, Hudi.

HUDI *looks at* RACHEL.

Oh, sorry.

Pause.

It's good to see you back.

HUDI (*not looking at* MICKY *or* RACHEL): Coming back, today. Just walking round. You know, they always say, the solidarity. I mean, you could cut it with a knife.

Pause. The music changes. A moment, then:

RACHEL: Hey, Hudi, d'you want a dance?

HUDI: No thanks. Have one with Micky.

MICKY: No, mate. don't want to leave you –

HUDI: 'S all right. I got my foaming brew for company.

RACHEL: Are you sure?

HUDI: Go on.

RACHEL (*stands*): All right. See you in a minute.

RACHEL *and* MICKY *go. Pause.* HUDI *drinks. Pause. Enter* GEORGE, *his coat slung over his shoulder.* HUDI *takes out a cigarette, feels in his pocket for matches. Hasn't got any.* GEORGE *takes out a lighter, lights* HUDI's *cigarette.* HUDI *looks up at* GEORGE.

GEORGE: Hallo, Hudi.

HUDI: Eh?

GEORGE: What's a charming place like this doing around a villain like you?

HUDI: Eh?

GEORGE: Sorry to interrupt your evening, but thought it best to do the job off the manor. East being a bit bubbly tonight. What with one working-class triumph and another.

HUDI: Who are you?

GEORGE: Leave it out, Hudi. You know who I am.

HUDI: No, I don't.

GEORGE *sits on a chair, the wrong way round.*

GEORGE: OK, Hudi. I'll play the game. (*He shows his warrant card.*)

HUDI: What's that?

GEORGE: It's a warrant card.

HUDI: What's a warrant card?

GEORGE: Hudi, do us a favour. I'm a copper and you're being nicked.

HUDI: Oh. I see.

GEORGE (*stands*): Linda done it, Hudi. We picks her up, leaking gear from every office, does a parish on your place and finds the Crown Jewels.

HUDI: You searched my flat?

GEORGE: Very lucky really. A bolt from the blue. Or, in this case, several bolts of blue.

Pause.

HUDI: I don't get –

GEORGE: It comes from Hong Kong. They ship it to Rotterdam, then fly it to Heathrow. Then somewhere between Number Two Terminal and its rightful destination, it gets spirited into your van. And then, by your good offices, its strewn up and down Commercial Street like confetti at a wedding.

Pause.

Call yourself Hudi? Need to be Houdini to get out of this one.

HUDI: It's straight. I bought it. Kosher.

GEORGE: Hudi, it's about as kosher as a bacon sandwich. Well, shall we toddle?

Pause.

It's your own fault, Hudi. You shouldn't go doing knuckle-jobs on your loved ones, should you?

HUDI, *angry, stands.*

Don't be melodramatic, Hudi, there's a love. Shall we go?

Pause. HUDI *knocks back his pint. They are just turning to go when* ANNA *enters. She's in her street clothes.* GEORGE *tactfully withdraws.* ANNA *sits at the table.*

ANNA (*to* HUDI, *firmly*): I've decided. You're right. I've jacked it in.

> HUDI *looks at her for a moment, then walks out, followed by* GEORGE. ANNA *amazed. Enter* MICKY *and* RACHEL. ANNA *looks at them.*

RACHEL (*surprised*): Where's Hudi?

Scene Twelve

Straight into the Law Locks Up song, during which the set is changed. HUDI *brings on his own chair and sits. He looks totally crushed.*

Law Locks Up

SONG:
The Law locks up
The man or woman
Who steals the goose
From off the common
But leaves the greater villain loose
Who steals the common from the goose

The Law demands
That we atone
When we take things we
Do not own
But leaves the lords and ladies fine
Who own things that are yours and mine

> *The song holds.* HUDI *looks up, suddenly, as if something has just struck him.*

HUDI: Hey. You. A'n't you missed something out?

> GEORGE *appears.*

GEORGE: Like what?

HUDI: A'n't you going to ask me who I'm working for? The big boys? Bosses? Eh?

> *Pause.*

GEORGE: Hudi. Now would I. Ask you to grass on your mates. I mean, now would I.

> *Pause. With supreme self-satisfaction:*

It's a bloody old system, Hudi.

> *Drum beat.* HUDI *and* GEORGE *off, as the next scene begins.*

Scene Thirteen

From either side, enter MICKY *and* RACHEL. RACHEL *carries two brown bags of groceries.*

MICKY: Bastards.

RACHEL: Who?

MICKY: The Filth. I just seen Hudi.

RACHEL: How is he?

MICKY: Sick. So'm I. (*Slight pause.*) They're just doing him. Not the blokes he's working for. Just him.

> *Slight pause.*

RACHEL: How'd they get on to him?

MICKY: Dunno. He didn't say. Look, you know Briant Colour Printing, the sit-in, lads who did the 'Five Out' posters. Well, they've asked a hand, picketing this paperworks, what forced their firm to close. And the Filth is spoiling for a bit of aggravation. So, I thought, go down. OK?

RACHEL: OK. We'll go.

MICKY: We?

RACHEL: Why not. After dinner, though. We got all this to get through.

MICKY (*going over*): Eh? (*He looks in the brown bags.*) Blimey. Where you get all that?

RACHEL: Well. You don't get strike pay, do you?

> MICKY *looks at* RACHEL.

Fell off the back of a trolley.

> *Drum beat.* RACHEL *and* MICKY *go, as the next scene begins.*

Scene Fourteen

Enter GEORGE. *He starts with bravado, but breaks down at the end.*

GEORGE: It was the 28th of July, the day after mobs of howling dockers had intimidated their delegates into calling an all-out strike. The dockers, having tasted blood, were determined further to wreak their venom on the rest of

the community, the weak and defenceless, those least able to stand up for themselves, in this case the Metropolitan Police Force.
It was the 28th of July. Acting in support of a mob of recently disemployed printing workers, the dockers formed a human wall in front of a Bermondsey paperworks, thus provoking the boys in blue into waiting till there was only fifty left, blocking the road, and coming down on them like a ton of cement.

Pause.

It was the 28th of July. Once again, events conclusively proved . . . The existence of a sinister conspiracy to . . .

Pause.

Villains, OK. Do villains. But not . . . Not women. Not blokes who . . .

The song cuts in – the final verse of Law Locks up – and during it GEORGE goes.

SONG:
The poor and wretched
Won't escape
If they conspire
The law to break
This will be so, while they endure
Those who conspire to make the law

The law locks up
The man or woman
Who steals the goose
From off the common
And geese will still a common lack
Until they go and steal it back.

Scene Fifteen

Enter MICKY. Behind him, the music grows from nothing.

MICKY: Down Pentonville. Actually, lot of the time, it got a bit depressing. Five days, nothing moving. But then, one day, we heard this sound, and couldn't work out what it was. And looked up the road, and heard the music, the band, and saw all the banners, and it was a march, with building workers, council workers, God knows who, black and white, the

lot, came marching up the road to Pentonville.

The song comes in. The whole company sings.

A Tale to Tell Your Children

SONG:
A tale to tell your children
Of 1972
When the dockers and the miners
Showed the world what they could do
They were up against the Tories
They proved to us at last
There is no prison strong enough
To hold the working class

Where were you
In '72
Where were we in '73
And '74
Easy
Easy
Easy to smash the law

A tale to tell your children
Of 1973
When Heath imposed a wage freeze
Not unsuccessfully
The gasmen and the porters
Were crushed beneath the law
He knew he'd won the battle
But he hadn't won the war

Where were you, *etc*

A tale to tell your children
Of 1974
The miners they came out again
And showed Ted Heath the door
They forced him out of office
And the working class has won
It is a noble victory
The struggle's just begun

Where were you, *etc*

At the end of the song, there is a sudden spot on a man in a tie. He is a MEMBER of Parliament.

MEMBER: On one thing we must, I think, be clear. We opposed the industrial policies of this Conservative Government. We support workers engaged in legitimate action against these policies.
But there are limits to the action we can support. As members of parliament, we must stand by the principle

that bad laws should be changed, not broken.
As a Shadow Cabinet, and, therefore, as a potential government, we cannot and must not countenance the flouting of the rule of law.

End of Act One

ACT TWO

"To secure for the workers by hand or by brain the full fruits of their industry and the most equitable distribution thereof that may be possible upon the basis of the common ownership of the means of production, distribution and exchange."

Section (4) of the
Labour Party Constitution.

"Our objective is to bring about a fundamental and irreversible shift in the balance of wealth and power in favour of working people and their families."

Labour Party General Election Manifesto,
October 1974

"Parliamentary democracy and the rule of law are inseparable."

Manifesto of the
Social Democratic Alliance, 1975

"The people of this country do not want more nationalisation. They recognise that we need an efficient and profitable private sector."

Manifesto of the
Social Democratic Alliance, 1975

"The state machine is neutral. It is like a car waiting to be driven. Whichever way it is steered, it will go."

Harold Wilson, 1964

ACT TWO
Scene One

Enter GEORGE in a spot. He wears a different raincoat. He smokes a cheroot. He speaks to the audience.

GEORGE: OK. Act Two Prologue. Fill you in.
Time: 1975. Harold Wilson is Prime Minister. Margaret Thatcher is the leader of the Opposition. The Queen is still the Queen.
Subject of story: Yet more conspiracies of various kinds to undermine our way of life and cherished liberties.
But I, am a different George. Occupation: Deputy Chief Reporter on the Weekly Journal incorporating the Argus and Bugle. A newshound. Scribe.
And, although the place is still the East End, it is a different East End. No longer that of working-class solidarity and tightly-knit communities. But that of Tower-Blocks and Re-development and Squatters and Things Falling Apart.
But then, you won't remember, will you, how it was. Before your time.

Folderol

SONG:
O I'll sing you a story
A tale I will tell
Of the days of me youth
In the sound of Bow Bells
We were po-or but honest
We suffered the cramp
For the feeling of fellowship
Hunger and damp

Chorus:
With a folderorol
And a folderolro
Wherever you wander
Where'er ye may go
With a folderolro
Back home you will come
Cos you know there's no place
Like a slum
Ti-um-tum

O it may have looked rough but
Twas cosy and nice
We were all in one room
Dad, Mum, Gran and the mice

And how far I may wander
I say as I roam
If you're going to get rickets
Then get 'em at home

Chorus

O they put us in blocks
Twenty storeys they climb
And our Gran's in a home and
Our Kid's doing time
With a tear in me eye
Of me old place I think
With its shops on the corner
And rats in the sink

Chorus

Scene Two

During the song, the scene is changed to a vegetable patch. RACHEL is working on it.

GEORGE: It is June 1975. The great British public has just referended the Common Market. And unemployment is 876,000, the Stock Exchange index is 331, the pound is worth two dollars twenty-seven, and inflation is twenty-three per cent. And unbeknownst to the Government, the Eurocrats, the Stock Exchange or the Gnomes of Zurich, a petty crook comes out of H.M.Prison Pentonville.

Enter HUDI with a pack of six cans of beer. Exit GEORGE.

HUDI: Hi, Rache.

RACHEL *looks up.*

RACHEL: Hudi.

HUDI: How you doing.

RACHEL (*stands*): You're out.

HUDI: That's right.

RACHEL (*goes to embrace HUDI, but realises she's covered in earth*): Oh, I'm . . . all filthy.

HUDI: Don't matter.

RACHEL *hugs HUDI.*

RACHEL: When d'you come out? You should have said.

HUDI: Well, di'n't want a great drama, did I. D'you want a drink?

RACHEL: Yuh. Lovely.

HUDI: Had a few already. First thing you want to do. Well, second thing, but a'n't managed to get that together yet.

They open their cans.

Told me you'd be down here. What you doing?

RACHEL: I'm growing caulis.

HUDI: Caulis?

RACHEL: That's right. You are looking at the Carter allotment.

HUDI: Round here used to be part of the Millwall, di'n'it?

RACHEL: That's right. Rich soil. (*Slight pause.*) Well. Cheers.

HUDI: Up yours.

They drink.

Micky?

RACHEL: Should be along. Comes down after his turn.

HUDI: Great.

Pause.

Well, tell us all about it.

RACHEL: 'Bout what?

HUDI: What's been happening. The dock strike.

RACHEL: Oh, well, you best ask Micky.

HUDI: Seemed from the papers, they did well.

RACHEL: Yuh, well, you best ask Micky.

Pause.

HUDI: Hey, knew something I wanted to know. Are the Shrewsbury pickets out?

RACHEL: No. They're not.

Pause. HUDI *is looking around.*
RACHEL *notices.*

What's the problem?

HUDI: Oh, um . . . see, trouble with being without the juice for three years is it does have a funny effect on your bladder.

RACHEL: Um . . . the river?

HUDI: Oh, fine. 'Scuse I.

Exit HUDI. RACHEL *goes back to her work. Enter* MICKY.

MICKY: Evening, Percy.

RACHEL: Hey, Micky, guess what.

MICKY: Give up.

RACHEL: Hudi's out of the nick

MICKY: What? Where is he?

RACHEL: Poisoning the fish.

MICKY: Eh?

HUDI (*off*): Micky. Micky! (*He re-enters.*) Mick.

MICKY: Hude.

HUDI: How's you?

MICKY: Fair to worse, and you?

HUDI: Fair to plastered, brother.

They assault each other merrily.

MICKY: When d'you get out?

HUDI: S'morning.

MICKY: You must come and stay, till you get sorted out.

RACHEL *looks up, but then back to her caulis.*

HUDI: Well, thanks a lot.

Pause.

MICKY: Ridiculous. Three years, and I can't think of anything to say.

HUDI: Well, tell us about the dock strike.

MICKY: What, you mean this recent one?

HUDI: That's right.

Pause.

MICKY: You ever come across the phrase a right fiasco?

Slight pause.

All right. The Great 1975 Dock Strike. Bloody containers again. Seeing as how, in '72, we'd managed to smash the Industrial Relations Act, but not the groupage. And, we start the picketing again, and four lads blossom a lorry and get took off pay, and out we come. Rock solid.

HUDI: That's good.

MICKY: Well, course it is. The only trouble being, a) it's only London, and b) the leadership don't lead. And we're out five weeks, get nothing, and go back with Jack Jones promising that Labour's Docks Bill's gonna bring the New Jerusalem. Well, so it may, but . . .

HUDI: Di'n't gain nothing.

MICKY: No. A tale not to tell your children.

Pause.

RACHEL: It's happening all over. Jobs going. Tate and Lyle, Standard Cables. You see, they got these grants, to move work to the north, and it's round here bears the brunt of it. I mean, it's great for people in Northumberland, but round here . . .

HUDI: Well, you ought to see your bloody MP 'bout that. After all, he is a Cabinet Minister.

RACHEL (*goes back to her veg*): Yuh. He is.

HUDI: Well?

MICKY: As such, he takes a wider view.

HUDI: What d'you mean?

MICKY: The good of the wider community.

HUDI: Don't get you.

MICKY: As he puts it, what's the transport system for.

Pause.

RACHEL: This place is dying. For us. You heard the tale, 'bout Taylor Woodrow. Bought up St Katherine's dock, on the promise they'd build some council housing. Well, we got the marina and the flashy hotel and the flats at twenty quid a day. What we i'n't got so far is a sign of a hint of a suggestion of one solitary house. For us. As lives here.

HUDI (*suddenly very angry*): Ought to do them bastards. Ought to do them.

Members of bleeding Parliament. We elected them. They a'n't got freehold on our bloody votes for life. (*He flings the beercan across the stage.* MICKY *and* RACHEL *look at him.*) Sorry. Think it's the booze. Straight to the head.

Pause.

RACHEL: There is, in fact, a way to do that bastard.

HUDI: Is there?

RACHEL: Yuh. Not noisy or spectacular. In fact, it's rather slow and quiet. (*She stands. To* HUDI:) The thing 'bout horticulture is, you got to have the patience, when you've sown the seed, to wait for things to grow.

Music. MICKY *goes.* RACHEL *and* HUDI *sing:*

The World Has Changed

HUDI: Since 1972
The world has changed
The vision through
The prison bars
Had such a rosy glow

RACHEL: Since 1972
It's re-arranged
That cosy view
Of yours and ours
It has just got to go

Other voices join RACHEL:

And if you think about it
Now the stakes are higher
Now we'll see what's true
Now we got the Tories out it's
Our lot that's in power
And we'll see what they can do

HUDI: In 1972
When I was here
It seemed so grand
So rough and tough
So tell me what went wrong

RACHEL: Since 1972
Things coming clear
A wage demand
Is not enough
Those happy days are gone

Other voices join RACHEL:

And if you think about it

Now the stakes are higher
Now we'll see what's true
Now we've got the Tories out it's
Our lot that's in power

And we'll see what *we* can do

Scene Three

A pool room in a pub. PAUL is playing. Enter GEORGE.

GEORGE: Paul Johnstone. 32 years of age. Stated occupation: polytechnic lecturer. Hobbies: the Cinema, chess and militant entryism. (*Helpfully:*) A bedsitter infiltrator. Johnny-come-lately-Trotskyist. Self-appointed samurai.

Enter HUDI.

And this one, you know.

HUDI: Paul Johnstone.

PAUL: Gerry Neill. (*He shakes HUDI's hand.*) I'm an armchair revolutionary.

HUDI: Oh, nice. I'm a mindless militant.

PAUL (*waving a cue*): You play?

HUDI (*taking it*): You bet.

GEORGE: The conspiracy is forged, in smoke-filled rooms behind closed doors.

HUDI turns towards the exit.

PAUL: Leave the door, mate, gets like an oven in here.

HUDI comes back.

GEORGE: In well-ventilated rooms behind half-open doors. (*He goes.*)

HUDI and PAUL shoot pool.

PAUL: You live in Timberton?

HUDI: That's right.

PAUL: You ever been in the Party before?

HUDI: No.

PAUL: OK. First of all, then, its weird and wonderful structure. (*As he shoots:*) A constituency Labour Party is run by a General Management Committee, consisting of delegates from various organisations. First. the branches. Second, the affiliated trade unions, and third, bits and pieces like young socialists, women and the Co-operative Party. Clear so far?

HUDI: It is.

PAUL: Good. Now, in this constituency, on all three fronts, things are moving. More unions affiliating. Branches growing. Places like Timberton, which up to now've been little more than the Chairman, his wife and his dog, expanding. As are the bits and pieces. We have, for instance, doubled the Co-op membership in the last three months. Still clear?

HUDI: As day.

PAUL: Right. Now, elections to the GMC take place in January. So what we want to do, is gain a majority at those meetings.

HUDI: Sorry, who's we?

PAUL: The small and unrepresentative clique of doctrinaire wildmen whose aim is to capture the Party for their own political ends.

HUDI: Oh. Yuh. 'Course. And then?

PAUL: The GMC changes colour.

HUDI: And then?

PAUL looks at HUDI, then back to the game. Quite quietly:

PAUL: You know, our member said he felt more in common with some liberals and Tories than with the Loonies Of The Left. Denied he was calling for a coalition. (*Slight pause.*) You know, this all started with the unions. Rank and file blokes, coming in, screaming angry with what he said 'bout Pentonville. (*Slight pause.*) And he says we're out of touch.

HUDI (*going to play*): Are you?

PAUL: You know, Gerry, when the Labour Party got its highest vote in history? In 1951. After six years of the most left-wing government we've ever had. You know the Tories highest vote this century? In 1959. When we were led by men of moderation and the centre.

HUDI: Question.

PAUL: Shoot.

HUDI: What you in it for?

PAUL: No secret. In it to transform the Party. In the short term, see that it's returned to those from whence it came. Not capture it, recapture it. They stole it. Steal it back.

GEORGE *has reappeared.*

HUDI: We'll say it, you know, fell –

PAUL *smiles.* HUDI *smiles.*

GEORGE: And thus, their machinations concluded, the conspirators –

PAUL (*interrupts, brightly, as he shoots*): Oh, just one little point, mate, while I think. If anyone wheels out the Trot clique bit, just remark how odd it is that when the Right's active it's healthy democracy, but when it's the Left it's a sinister conspiracy. Right?

HUDI: Right.

GEORGE: Right.

Scene Four

This scene is bounded by the Recruitment Song, and the little scenes weave in and out rapidly. The RECRUITEES *are various, and could be drawn from members of the band.*

Recruitment Song
PAUL: Would you like to join the Labour Party
We're recruiting in this town
RACHEL: Why not come and join the Labour Party
Can I say I'll put you down
RECRUITEE: I dunno they seem cut off they don't
Appear to do that much for me
HUDI: 'Course that's true, but get involved,
Turn up and vote and brother then you'll see

RECRUITEE: OK OK
Where do I sign
RACHEL: OK Today
Right there on the line

The Minister
is asked if he'll oppose the EEC
The Minister
informs us that it's best for you and me

GEORGE: July 1975. Unemployment nudging the million, and the pound is two dollars fourteen.

HUDI *is working out something on a calculator. He has a list. Enter* PAUL.

PAUL: Gerry.

HUDI: Paul. I nearly done it. Branches, works out now, they should have twenty-four delegates, and we should have – um – (*Last figure. In triumph:*) – one hundred and sixty.

PAUL *looks, takes the calculator, does a quick calculation.*

PAUL: Um – sixteen.

HUDI: Sixteen?

PAUL: That's right.

Back into SONG as they break:

RACHEL: Would you like to join the Labour Party
Would you like to take a stand
PAUL: If you come and join the Labour Party
We can build a better land
RECRUITEE: Come on, mate, they say one thing,
And then in power see the things they do
RACHEL: That's because it's run by blokes
Like Healey, and it isn't run by you

RECRUITEE: OK OK
Where do I sign
RACHEL: OK Today
Right there on the line

The Minister
is asked about the pickets in the nick
The Minister
informs us in the nick they'll have to stick

GEORGE: November 1975

PAUL *and* HUDI *meet.* PAUL *holding a manuscript.*

PAUL: Gerry.

HUDI: Paul.

PAUL: Your leaflet. If you don't mind, I've made a couple of alterations.

HUDI (*grabs the manuscript*): Yuh? What's this? What's wrong with that?

PAUL: It's ungrammatical. You've split an infinitive.

HUDI: Look, mate, when I split an infinitive, it stays split.

PAUL: Oh, I'm . . . Sorry I . . .

HUDI (*striding off*): So I should bleeding well think.

HUDI *comes back on again with a* RECRUITEE.

HUDI: Would you like to join the Labour Party
Come on, darling, move your arse
Why not come and force the Labour Party
To support the working class
RECRUITEE: Hey are you a Trot like I have read of
In the Mirror and the Mail
HUDI: Look, love, for them sods, you're not Roy
Jenkins and you're way beyond the pale

RECRUITEE: OK OK
Where do I sign
HUDI: OK Today
Right there on the line

The Minister
is asked about the million on the dole
The Minister
informs us they must stay out in the cold

GEORGE: January 1976.

HUDI *on one side, standing;* RACHEL *centre; and* MRS WILLIS, *a social democrat, standing on the other.*

MRS WILLIS: My name is Emma Willis, and I am seeking the privilege of serving you as Secretary of the Timberton Branch of the Constituency Labour Party.

HUDI: My name is Gerry Neill, I'm running for branch secretary, and I don't intend to lose.

MRS WILLIS *looks at* HUDI.

RACHEL: For Willis? For Neill?

Pause.

MRS WILLIS: Oh.

HUDI: We shall now commence the construction of the socialist order.

RACHEL: Would you like to join the Labour Party
If you did it would be great
PAUL: Why not come and join the Labour Party
HUDI: And we'll overthrow the state
RECRUITEE: Oh come on brother all them buggers
They are far too gone to re-arrange
PAUL: That is what they hope you'll say
But if you join with us it's going to change

RECRUITEE: OK OK
Where do I sign
PAUL: OK Today
PAUL/RACHEL: Right there on the line

The Minister
is asked about the spending cuts he's made
The Minister
informs us that it's best for British trade

GEORGE: February 1976. Unemployment, 1,304,000. And the pound is two dollars two.

PAUL *with a list.* HUDI *and* RACHEL.

PAUL: Right. Beckley. Six delegates.

HUDI: Ours.

PAUL: Selby South. Two delegates.

RACHEL: Theirs.

PAUL: Selby North. Ten.

HUDI: Theirs.

PAUL: Branwell Park, eight, Collet Marsh, four.

RACHEL: Ours.

PAUL: Stonewood, four.

HUDI: Theirs.

PAUL: And Timberton, ours, twelve.

RACHEL: Thirty. Sixteen.

HUDI: It's in the bag.

ALL THREE: Would you like to join the Labour Party
And together we will win
If you come and join the Labour Party

We can change it from within

RECRUITEE: What's the point when
we are stuck with
someone like our present duff MP

HUDI: Well, between ourselves, I rather
think
That that will not for ever be

RECRUITEE: OK OK
Where do I sign
ALL THREE: OK Today
Right there on the line.

Scene Five

Enter GEORGE. *During his speech, a
pub table and three chairs are set up.*
GEORGE's *glass of scotch is on the
table.*

GEORGE: It is September 1976.
Unemployment is nearly up to one and
a half million and the pound is nearly
down to one dollar seventy. And this is
the Labour Club, and, in an upstairs
room, the General Management
Committee is meeting to consider
whether to hold a Special General
Management Committee Meeting to
consider whether to dump their MP.
And I'm skulking round, my nose
poised and twitching, eager for a sniff
of a –

A door slams.

Oho.

PAUL *strides in, followed by* HUDI.

HUDI: All right, Paul, but the point is –

PAUL (*turns back, aggressively*): What
do you want to drink?

HUDI (*aggressively*): A pint of synthetic
bitter, please.

PAUL (*going out*): Right. Then.

GEORGE *catches* HUDI. MRS
WILLIS *is entering behind.*

GEORGE: Excuse me, I'm from the
Journal, and I wonder –

HUDI: Get knotted. (*He goes.*)

GEORGE *turns, to confront the
grinning* MRS WILLIS.

GEORGE: Ah. Mrs Willis.

MRS WILLIS: Mr West.

GEORGE: Looking, were that possbile,
even lovelier than ever.

MRS WILLIS: Looking, were that
possible, even greasier than usual.

GEORGE: Shall we sit?

MRS WILLIS: Charmed, I'm sure.

They sit at the table, GEORGE
writing in his notebook.

GEORGE: Well?

MRS WILLIS: Meeting suspended.

GEORGE: Why?

MRS WILLIS: Irregularities.

GEORGE: About?

MRS WILLIS: Delegates' credentials.

GEORGE: Whose.

MRS WILLIS: Theirs.

GEORGE: Blokes through there?

MRS WILLIS: Correct.

GEORGE: Who are?

MRS WILLIS: Paul Johnstone with tie,
Gerry Neill without.

BERNIE, *Party Chairperson, has
entered.*

GEORGE: And which –

BERNIE: Well, hallo, George.

GEORGE: Bernie. How's it going.

BERNIE (*sits between them*): Well, a
hard grind, George, chairing this
committee, lively, buoyant with democratic controversy, everyone their axe
to grind, and leaking like a colander.

GEORGE: I beg your pardon?

BERNIE: Di'n't know you knew George,
Mrs W.

MRS WILLIS: Oh, we don't know each
other well.

BERNIE: Let's keep it that way, eh?
(*He draws a handwritten paper from
his pocket.*)

GEORGE: Do I see a statement,
Bernie?

BERNIE: Yes, you do. An official
statement.

Long pause. MRS WILLIS *stands.*

MRS WILLIS: Well. Perhaps. My bedtime.

GEORGE: Goodnight, Mrs Willis.

MRS WILLIS: Goodnight, Mr West. Bernie. (*She goes.*)

BERNIE: Right. (*He reads out the statement;* GEORGE *takes notes.*) At Wednesday night's meeting of the GMC, certain charges were made concerning alleged irregularities in the election of delegates from certain affiliated organisations. It was resolved to suspend the meeting until these charges have been thoroughly investigated. (*He folds the paper.*)

GEORGE: That's it?

BERNIE: That's it.

GEORGE: Which organisations?

BERNIE: Do us a favour, George.

GEORGE: Bernie, if I don't get any more than this –

BERNIE: Mm?

GEORGE: I'll have to give Mrs W. a tinkle, won't I?

Pause.

BERNIE: Timberton branch. And a counter-charge from the left against the Fabians. That's all I'm saying.

GEORGE: Uh, Bernie –

BERNIE: George, I said –

GEORGE: Which side you on?

Slight pause.

BERNIE: I'm on the side that wins.

BERNIE *leaves, passing the entering* RACHEL.

Hallo, Mrs Carter.

BERNIE *has gone.* GEORGE *downs his scotch, catches up with* RACHEL, *who's crossing to go out following* PAUL *and* HUDI.

GEORGE: Evening, Mrs Carter, West, the Journal, and I wonder –

RACHEL: Get knotted. (*She goes.*)

GEORGE (*out front*): You know, some-

times I think about doing a job that's a bit more popular. You know, like a traffic warden or a tax collector or a public hangman, something like that.

He goes, as PAUL, HUDI *and* RACHEL *enter and go to table and sit.*

PAUL: Right. Go through it, point by point. One. Three members of Timberton Branch under fifteen years of age, contrary to Rule Three, section three. True?

HUDI: Well . . . sort of.

PAUL: Sort of?

HUDI: True.

PAUL: Two. Four members not resident in Britain for one year, contrary to the same rule. True?

HUDI: Well, kind of . . .

PAUL: Kind of?

HUDI: True.

PAUL: Three. April meeting of the branch. Held at the required two weeks' notice for people you thought'd vote your way, and three days for everyone else. True?

HUDI: Trueish.

PAUL: Ish?

HUDI: Postal delay?

PAUL *shakes his head.*

True. And actually –

PAUL: Yes?

HUDI: There's a dozen under fifteen. Another eight haven't been here long enough. And I'd like those offences to be taken into account when passing –

PAUL: Gerry –

HUDI: Oh, leave it out, they do the same. And what about those bleeding Cambridge students who suddenly appeared from out of thin air. Five-star infiltrators?

PAUL: Oh, fine, sure, we can fight it like that, on a cloak-and-dagger level, go through their lists, check who's not a resident, who's not in their proper union, who don't pay their political levy, all that. Can do. But we could have fought it properly, on the politics, till you broke the rules.

HUDI: Rules! What started this, eh? It started when our Member of Parliament said as how the dockers and the builders what got nicked should stay inside 'cos They Had Broke the Rules.

Pause.

Transform the sodding Labour Party. The Rulebook Road to Revolution.

Pause. PAUL *says nothing.*

RACHEL: We ought to stop post-morteming. Talk about what we got to do. Fix up a meeting.

PAUL: Yuh.

HUDI(*after a moment, brightly*): So, when shall we three meet again, In thunder, lightning or in rain?

PAUL: Eh?

HUDI: Macbeth. School play. I was third witch and bleeding magic.

RACHEL: Beg pardon?

HUDI (*direct to* PAUL, *with great charm*): And second murderer.

Scene Six

Bare stage. Enter ANNA.

ANNA: Anna. Revolutionary student and sometime lager salesperson. Graduated in 1974, and decided to become a radical campaigning journalist. Turned down by the Guardian. Decided to become a campaigning journalist. Turned down by the Sunday Times. Decided to become a journalist. And ended up on the Journal.

Enter GEORGE.

GEORGE: Annabelle, my sweetling.

ANNA: Yes, George?

GEORGE: A joblet.

ANNA: What might that be, George?

GEORGE: A little dig. Bloke I want to know about. One Gerry Neill. At present, something in the Timberton Branch of the Labour Party. Can do?

ANNA: No, George.

GEORGE: Whyever not, my casket?

ANNA: Well, for one, I'm busy on my squatting feature –

GEORGE: Ah, your squatting feature –

ANNA: And, two, feefifofum, I smell the blood of a witch-hunting man.

GEORGE: Oh, now, Anna, my honey-bun, whatever could have –

ANNA: George.

GEORGE: My joy?

ANNA: Get knotted. (*Exit* ANNA.)

GEORGE: What we call in the trade a committed. Graduate, of course. Personally, I blame free orange juice.

LINDA *enters to a mike, as* GEORGE *wanders off, muttering*:

Fee fi fo fum . . .

LINDA (*into the mike*): Linda.

Scene Seven

Music. During the song, a squatted house is set.

Linda's Song
LINDA:
She was
nearly twenty
She was Gerry's woman
No not Gerry's woman
Gerry's bird

She was
elementary
Look what she was given
Took what she was given
Not a word

Then she
gets done
Red-wristed with the booty
And the twelve months on probation
And she flew
Linda
moved on
Falling angel through the city
Through more kinds of habitation
Than she knew

She was a victim
all along the line
She is a story for our time

She is
twenty-three now
Given up on hoping
Taken up with coping
On the floor

She has
got the key now
And a great deal older
And a great deal colder
than before

And she
comes here
To an empty house in Stepney
Lives on what the State is giving
Does it well
Linda's
Three years
Through the maze of London's homeless
Through the haze of half-light living
What the hell

She was a victim
drained the bitter cup
Drained it and it Grew Her Up

*The song ends. A loud banging.
LINDA goes to a window, calls down.*

LINDA: Yuh? What you want?

ANNA (*off*): From the Journal.
Arranged to come and see you.

LINDA: Oh. Right. Look, door's
blocked up. Downstairs window on the
left. I'll come down. OK?

ANNA (*off*): OK.

*Exit LINDA. Pause. Thump. Pause.
Re-enter LINDA with ANNA, holding
one of her shoes, which has broken.*

LINDA: Sorry 'bout that.

ANNA: It's all right. Old pair.

LINDA: What you want, then?

ANNA: I'm doing a feature on squatting.

LINDA: You ought to see Zinneman.

ANNA: Who?

LINDA: He's the boss round here. Got
all the facts and figures. And opinions.
And all that.

ANNA: Is he in?

LINDA: No, he's occupying an embassy
this morning. Back later.

ANNA: Can I talk to you?

LINDA: If you like.

ANNA (*starting her notes*): What's your
name.

LINDA: Linda Barratt. Sit down.

ANNA (*sitting*): Thanks.

LINDA: I'd offer you some tea, but they
just cut the water off.

ANNA: Oh, I'm sorry.

LINDA: Yuh. Right charmers. They're
also planning concreting the drains.
Good thing you came today, stunk out
in a week. Still, look on the bright
side. Fact the street's empty, 'part
from us, means i'n't no vigis.

ANNA: Vigis?

LINDA: Vigilantes. Honest decent
citizens outraged by the layabouts and
scroungers.

ANNA (*takes a grubby leaflet from her
bag and reads*): 'The most important
element of the present attack on
squatting is that it is directed primarily
against that significant minority who
view squatting as a political act, a way
of life, an undermining of the fascist
straitjacket of the pig-state bourgeois
death-ethic . . .'

LINDA (*interrupts*): Yuh. That's
Zinneman. What you might call a dis-
tinctive prose style.

ANNA (*grins*): Yuh.

LINDA (*quite firmly*): There's also a
significant majority what squats 'cos
they can't get anywhere to live.
Actually, I don't see them as contradictory.

ANNA: But the people who own the
houses, the vigis, they don't see your
common interest.

LINDA: Oh, yuh, well. That's your great
British working class, i'n'it.

ANNA: How did you get into all this?

LINDA: Me? Personally? Well. (*She

perambulates.) OK. Linda's sorry tale. Deserted by her slobbish lover in 1972, leaving her nothing but a few bruises, a scar on the left arm that still a'n't gone, and a load of bent gear for the handling of which she gets probation. Quits her –

ANNA: Sorry, your bloke went inside?

LINDA: Yuh, did. Three years. So, quits her job in London's famous East End's famous Rag Trade –

ANNA: Sorry, so he'd be out now?

LINDA: Yuh, I s'pose he would. Anyway, then she goes on the SS, various problems, often of a cohabitationary character, and ends –

ANNA: Sorry, have you been in touch?

LINDA: With Hudi? Have I hell. So, anyway, she ends up here, squatting in wretchedness and –

ANNA: Hudi?

LINDA: The slob. A joke – Yehudi, on the fiddle. Get it?

Pause.

ANNA: I thought so. We have met.

LINDA: We have?

ANNA: Years ago, a pub. I was selling papers. He was there.

LINDA: You're right. And, yuh, that's shit-face.

ANNA: Don't think I ever got his real name.

LINDA: It's Gerry Neill.

Pause.

ANNA: I'm sorry?

LINDA: Gerry Neill.

Long pause. ANNA stands, not knowing what to do.

Anything the matter?

Pause. ANNA takes a decision.

ANNA: Oh, what the hell. Tell me all about him.

Music. ANNA and LINDA sing:

Sob Story

LINDA: Well, what you want to ask me And I'll tell you what I can

ANNA: Oh, just a bit of background About him, as a man

LINDA: I mean, fact, he was a slob But he had a lot of charm, you see

ANNA: Philanderer

LINDA: He was worried 'bout his job And I s'pose he took it out on me

ANNA: Took it out on her

Chorus:
ANNA: Story
Sob story
A glorious gory story
A darn good yarn
A right little tale
Story
Sob story

LINDA: Course the bugger had his background
His dad, you know, his mum

ANNA: His father beat his mother
He was dragged up in a slum

LINDA: I dunno what I done
Perhaps I hadn't been too nice

ANNA: No reason or rhyme

LINDA: And you mustn't get it wrong
It only happened once or twice

ANNA: From time to time

ANNA: *Chorus*

LINDA: I mean I thought of leaving
He could be a lot of fun

ANNA: She stuck with him though thick and thin
Despite the things he'd done

LINDA: Look you gotta understand
He thought his job was under threat

ANNA: He was employed?

LINDA: I mean mostly he was grand
But occasionally he got upset

ANNA: He was paranoid

GEORGE *joins them.*

ANNA/GEORGE: *Chorus*

All hold. HUDI appears, in a spot, out front.

HUDI: I'm sorry. Well, I mean, I'm dreadful sorry. You know, 'bout the loss of a halo. You know, 'bout the fact I'm not a bleeding saint (*He goes.*)

Reprise of Sob Story:

ANNA/GEORGE: Story
Sob Story

Scene Eight

RACHEL *is standing one side, holding a
newspaper. MICKY is on the other,
holding two big full bags. In the middle is
some kind of receptacle or basket.*

RACHEL: Bastards.

MICKY: Yuh.

RACHEL: And bastard.

MICKY: Eh?

RACHEL: Hudi.

MICKY: Oh, yuh.

Pause.

RACHEL: I mean, I'd just read some of
it. And Paul says, how people been
ringing, worried 'bout their vote, you
know? And I said, oh, we're being
very moral, i'n't we, just 'cos he's
done a bit of bird, he ought to
bleeding sue them. And he said, I'd
read the rest if I were you.

Pause.

I mean, I really didn't know, he
practised his karate on her person.
And the other stuff. Heathrow. I
mean, it all comes out, the dirty
denim, dunnit.

Pause.

Then, you dunno what to do. Whose
side you're on. I mean, it just divides –

MICKY: Think that is the idea.

Pause.

In '72, we closed the lie-factory.
Printers came out, and stopped the
papers.

RACHEL: Well, we can't –

MICKY: No, course you can't. (*Slight
pause. MICKY goes to RACHEL.
Quite forcefully:*) Pity 'bout the caulis.
But with the drought and all, a bit
exposed. Your 'taters, on the other
hand, have more protection. (*He pours
the bags, which contain potatoes, into*

the receptacle.) A'n't they.

*An instrumental reprise of Law Locks
Up covers the scene change.*

Scene Nine

*Foyer of the Journal. A table with news-
papers in binders. A counter at the side.
LINDA crosses to the counter, presses
the bell. No response. She presses again
and keeps pressing till the RECEP-
TIONIST arrives.*

RECEPTIONIST: Can I help you?

LINDA: Anna Lawrence.

RECEPTIONIST: Who shall I say is
calling?

LINDA (*tapping side of her nose*): Say
it's Deep Throat.

RECEPTIONIST: Certainly.

*The RECEPTIONIST goes. LINDA
sits, puts her feet up, picks up a bound
paper, reads. Enter ANNA.*

ANNA: Hallo, are you for me?

LINDA *puts down the paper.*

Oh. What do you want?

LINDA: What d'you reckon.

ANNA: Well, I assume it's to do with
the article.

LINDA: Right first time.

Pause.

ANNA: I suppose I was a little naive. I
didn't realise quite how it would be
used. You see, most of it was from the
cuttings.

LINDA: You didn't think how it'd be
used.

ANNA: Well, not –

LINDA: How bloody stupid.

Pause.

ANNA: I tried to put your side of it

LINDA: My side?

ANNA: That's right, the way I saw it –

LINDA: My side, as against whose?

ANNA: His.

LINDA: Oh, I see. With you. You mean, put my side, heartwarming tale of little flimsy creature victimised by brutish hulk. Sort of Bill Sykes stuff. Kind of, feminist line. Battered wives, that sort of angle.

ANNA: Well, I had got the impression –

LINDA: Impression?

ANNA: From our conversation –

LINDA: My dad was a slob.

ANNA: Sorry?

LINDA: My father was a dirty old slob. An idle old soak. He was a classic. His attitude to women compared un-favourably with that of Henry the Eighth. He had quadruple standards. He last did the washing up in 1959. And cruel with it, hour after hour, he'd dribble spite. And Mum, course, didn't say a word.

An ANGRY MAN *has walked in. He crosses to the counter. He rings the bell.*

And we thought he was a right old bastard. And when he fell ill, I mean he had the lot, heart, bronchitis, various unmentionables, we all thought good. Blessed release.

The MAN *is listening.* ANNA *aware, and occasionally looking round ner-vously.*

But then he wouldn't die. He hung on, week after month, sloshing about in his own juice, gripping on to life, like he was drowning, strangling it, hands round its neck. As he melted away like a plastic cup on a stove. (*Referring to the* MAN *at the counter:*) And don't bother 'bout him. It's not your dad I'm talking about.

The MAN *presses the bell again.*

And reason he hung on was revenge. 'Gainst us all, the lot, his shitty awful life. He lay there, stewed in shit, and grit his teeth, and said, I'll show them. The only thing he had was shouting at my mum. The only thing he could con-trol, and have a little power over. Breathing space. And so he kept on breathing it. Long as he could. Does that mean anything to you?

The MAN *presses the bell again.*

ANNA: I s'pose, you mean –

LINDA: I mean, leave us alone.

The RECEPTIONIST *appears.*

RECEPTIONIST: Can I help you.

MAN: Pick the Spot.

RECEPTIONIST: I beg your pardon?

MAN: I wish to query the result of last week's Pick the Spot.

Loudly, LINDA *gets up and goes, bumping into* GEORGE *as he comes in. The* MAN *turns, waves his paper at them.*

MAN: I was there, you see. I saw it.

GEORGE (*to* ANNA): Who was that?

ANNA: Linda Barratt. Dissatisfied cus-tomer.

GEORGE: Silly cow.

MAN: I was there.

GEORGE (*turns out front*): They wouldn't buy it if they didn't want to read it, would they? Don't blame me. Don't blame the bleeding scribe.

And into the Scribes song. Until her verse, ANNA *stays sitting, discon-solate. The* RECEPTIONIST *and the* ANGRY MAN *go.*

Scribes

GEORGE:
You will hear people say
The papers are trivial and low
The press is the same every day
They don't say what people should know
I will tell you my views
I have a simple creed
People are reading the news
News is what people will read

You say that opinion's not free
My answer is, button your lip
For competition will see
All views get a crack of the whip
I will give you my line
I will say how it is
If you don't like what's in mine
Then go out and read it in his

Exit GEORGE.

ANNA:
People tend to buy the gear

That the advertising business
wants to sell them
People tend to want to hear
What the people on the papers
want to tell them

Scribes
Scribes
Scribes

Scene Ten

*Committee room. BERNIE and the
PARTY SECRETARY behind a table.
An empty chair nearby. OTHERS,
including RACHEL, PAUL and MRS
WILLIS, around. GEORGE out front.*

GEORGE: The 10th of November, 1976.
Unemployment 1,387,000, inflation 16
per cent, the Stock Exchange 403, and
the pound is one fifty-seven. And the
reconstituted GMC meets to decide the
fate of the Member.

Indicating the empty chair:

The Member sits alone. (*He goes.*)

BERNIE: Brothers and sisters. Can we
make a start.

Pause.

Right. First, any apologies?

SECRETARY: Apologies have been
received from Brothers Lester, Newton,
McShane, Warner and Neill; and
Sisters Lovell and Wilson.

MRS WILLIS: Point of order, Mr Chairman.

BERNIE: Mrs Willis.

MRS WILLIS: Brother Neill. Since,
events, is Brother Neill still a delegate? I was under the impression he'd
resigned.

RACHEL: Brother Chairman, Brother
Neill was duly elected as a delegate
from the Co-operative Party.

MRS WILLIS: Point of order, is that
permissible under rule –

RACHEL: Point of order yes of course
it's bloody permissible, what about
Jack Steadley and the Fabians –

BERNIE: Sisters – I appreciate this is a
matter of principle –

RACHEL: And Stonewood, eight of
your members miraculously paying
subs from beyond the grave –

BERNIE: But as Brother Neill is not
here might I suggest –

MRS WILLIS: It is important, Mr
Chairman, to establish –

BERNIE: Of course it's important.
Everything's important. So too is
making it to the pub.

Pause. Benignly:

Now, come on. Let's all try and be
reasonable. It's going to be a long
night. Can I please call, proposer of
the motion.

And into the song:

Who is the Labour Party For?

SONG:
The Left began by saying,
We're not shirkers
We got this bloke elected
We're the workers
It's us who toils our balls off
At the poll
It's us should guard the Party's
Life and soul

Who is the Labour Party for
Who is the Labour Party for
Party of the future
Party of the past
Party of consensus
Party of a class
The question to answer today
Whose party is this, anyway?

MRS WILLIS: The Moderates then rose
To tell their story
RACHEL: That rose's other name
Should be, a Tory
MRS WILLIS: The issue is, whose MP
Should he be
The voters or the
Party GMC?

SONG: Who is the Labour Party, *etc.*

SONG: The Right spoke in the interests
Of the nation
The Left said we must make
A transformation

PAUL: The Minister replied to
What he'd heard
For half an hour,
Didn't say a word

SONG: But, who is the Labour Party,
etc.

The song ends. The SECRETARY,
*who had left, returns with a piece of
paper and gives it to* BERNIE, *who
reads. Pause.*

BERNIE: Brothers and sisters, could we
come back to order. We have a result.

Pause.

This vote, I would make clear, has
been counted and recounted.

Pause.

There were, you may like to know,
four spoiled ballot papers.

SOMEONE: Get on with it, Bernie!

BERNIE: I beg your pardon. 39 for, 39
against.

Pause.

That's a tie.

Pause.

And under standing orders, I'm afraid,
that means . . .

Long pause. BERNIE *turns to the
empty chair.*

Coalition talk. Forgive you anything
but that.

Out front:

40/39. The motion's carried.

The MEMBER's *chair falls over back-
wards. Pause.* MRS WILLIS *coughs.
They all look at her.*

MRS WILLIS: The Minister . . . asked
me to inform the meeting . . . that he
had to leave as soon as the business
was concluded, to attend a vital divi-
sion in the House.

BERNIE: I see.

MRS WILLIS (*suddenly, addressing the
audience*): You know, all I want is a
society of tolerance and decency and
mutual respect. With no extremes of
poverty. Where people work together.
All I want. I want it how it was.

Scene Eleven

At once, a big drum roll. MRS WILLIS
goes. RACHEL *and* PAUL *come forward, as if to sing a song. They are
interrupted by the entrance of* HUDI, *in
his overcoat. The drum roll cuts out.*

HUDI: Sorry to butt in. Was at home,
listening to the radio. Something, you
might want to know.
The Docks Labour Bill, you know, it
got amended in the Lords, to make it
a half mile corridor for dockwork,
'stead of five miles. Bloody ridiculous.
Anyway, Bill comes back to the
Commons tonight, for them to change
it back to what it was. Well, as it fell
out . . . it wasn't changed back. As it
fell out, two Labour MPs abstained,
and the bugger's fallen. Just thought
you might like to know.

PAUL: That must have been, after the
meeting, he rushed off to the House.

HUDI: Hardly worth it, just to abstain,
was it. Well, I'll be –

RACHEL: Hudi, d'you want a drink?

HUDI: No, I don't think so. I done bird,
see, not a pleasant class of bloke to
know.

Slight pause.

Anyway. I got a little job to do.

HUDI *goes as, at once, the music
comes in and* RACHEL *moves to the
mike. Her reprise of Who is the Labour
Party For covers the change.*

RACHEL: And I thought, we done the
job
Seemed elementary
We climbed the party ladder
We forced entry
But behind the window
There's another wall
Was there any point in
Entering at all?

What can the Labour Party do
What can it do for me and you

Party of elections
Breaking down the doors
Party passing statutes
Party making laws
The question to be answered, right now
Can the Party change things anyhow?

Scene Twelve

The MEMBER, *in a dressing gown over suit trousers and shirt. He sits at a table with a dictaphone. Starts it. We hear his voice.*

VOICE: And finally, my friends, I would ask you to be realistic. We social democrats –

Bell. He stops the machine. Bell again, longer. He goes out. Pause. He re-enters with HUDI.

MEMBER: Have you any idea what time it is?

HUDI: It's a long walk.

MEMBER: I thought you drove a van.

HUDI: I did.

MEMBER: Why have you come?

HUDI: I wanted to see the whites of your eyes.

Pause.

MEMBER: You've seen them already. Several times. There was a witty piece in the Guardian about our first meeting. I said, thanks for all the work you're doing, I do hope you're not involved with these extremists. You said, hmm.

HUDI: I haven't seen them, since.

MEMBER: True. Well, here they are, either side of my nose, and now perhaps –

HUDI: Bastard.

MEMBER: Why?

HUDI: Abstaining.

MEMBER: What?

HUDI: You abstained and killed the Docks Bill. Why? Spite?

MEMBER: But I didn't.

HUDI: Eh?

MEMBER: My dear old Gerry, I didn't abstain. I voted with the Government.

Pause.

HUDI: But, you, you don't want the Bill, do you?

MEMBER: Not a lot, no.

HUDI: Oh, blimey. The man of principle.

MEMBER: There's a principle called collective cabinet responsibility.

HUDI: Yuh, like there's a principle of doing what your local Party wants.

MEMBER: I think that's where we get on to small and unrepresentative cliques out of touch with the views of the vast majority.

HUDI: Yuh, like the Cabinet.

Pause. The MEMBER *laughs.*

MEMBER: Look, can I get you a drink? Or would that go against your righteous pride?

HUDI: I'll have an extremely large whisky.

MEMBER: Good. (*Exit. He calls from off:*) You do realise, of course, about tonight, that it was the Lords' fault. They shot down the Bill. Our two kamikaze pilots just stopped us picking it up again. (*He reappears, hands* HUDI *a whisky.*)

HUDI: Yuh. There was one of them, one of his lordships, claimed dockers steal a third of the cargo they handle. That's eleven million tons a year, and works out at twenty tons a docker a week. Not counting sickness and holidays.

MEMBER: There was a joke going round that a confrontation between the Lords and the dockers was rather appropriate. Both being small groups of reactionaries whose entitlements are passed down from father to son.

HUDI: There is a difference, of course.

MEMBER: What's that?

HUDI: The dockers work.

MEMBER (*laughing*): Well done.

HUDI: Don't patronise me.

MEMBER: I wouldn't dream of it.

Pause.

HUDI: You've no idea, have you, what's happened to me.

MEMBER: You've no idea, have you, what's happened to me.

Slight pause.

HUDI: Oh, yuh. You've really got bother. I mean you only got the Government, the Tories, the press on your side, I mean –

MEMBER: Oh no.

HUDI: What you mean, no?

MEMBER: I mean, there you've got it wrong. I'm going to be dumped. (*Slight pause.*) In time. I mean, they'll make their statements, for a bit, in my support. But even now, already, in the House, I sit alone in the tea room.

HUDI: Well, poor old you.

MEMBER: A decent interval, then I'll be dumped from the Cabinet. Actually, I might resign. Either way, I shall be a sacrificial victim. Just like you. We're both embarrassments, and both of us will have to go. Because we undermine the myth.

HUDI: What's that?

MEMBER: This Great Movement Of Ours. This great coalition of the Left and Right. This Labour Party, great because of not despite its disagreements. All those myths. Both you and I prove that there are sides, opposed and contradictory, and someday they'll have to fight it out, and one of them will win and one of them will lose. They know that, but they don't want to know. So those who tell them – chop. Like us. Your health.

Pause.

I don't know why I'm being cheerful. I've just lost my job.

HUDI: I didn't have a job to lose.

MEMBER: That's true. (*Slight pause.*)

Well, here we are, two implacable foes, fighting cocks, and yet we're getting on rather well. I think that says something or another –

HUDI (*interrupts*): Do you really stand for anything?

MEMBER: Oh, yes.

HUDI: Like what?

MEMBER: The Rule of Law

HUDI: Oh, yuh, remember –

MEMBER: And I'll tell you why. Because there's three ways you can run society. By money and wealth, as the Tories do. By force of numbers and industrial strength, as the militants would argue. And, for us, in the middle, Tribune Group as well, by using law. The law: a kind of no-man's land between the armies. Kind of barbed wire, slung around, protecting it. And if you believe in that middle ground –

HUDI: Do you?

MEMBER: Do I what?

HUDI: Believe in the middle ground.

MEMBER: I've just lost my job for the cause of the middle ground.

HUDI: That doesn't answer the question.

Pause. Angry:

I mean, you said, the Tories couldn't give a toss, they'll break any laws you make, they'll use the House of Lords and the Stock Exchange and the bloody army, so it is kind of important to know if your precious middle ground in fact exists at all.

Pause.

I asked a question!

Pause.

MEMBER: All right. I'll even answer it.

The MEMBER goes to the dictaphone, switches it on. We hear his VOICE.

VOICE: And finally, my friends, I would ask you o be realistic. We social democrats believe that in time of prosperity it is possible to remove inequality and injustice by transferring the surplus of wealth produced from the rich to the poor. But that depends on having prosperity and having a surplus. We are now having to choose – and that's what the debate on public spending is about – between social goals and the health of the wealth-making machine. Put simply, we have to choose between the interests of the needy and the interests of profitable industry. As the former depends on the latter, we really have no choice. (*He switches off the machine.*)

MEMBER: I think that means, the answer's no.

HUDI: I'm going.

MEMBER: How are you getting home?

HUDI: Same way I came.

MEMBER: Don't be ridiculous. Let me ring you a cab.

HUDI *looks at him, then he goes out. The* MEMBER *shrugs. To the dictaphone. Records:*

We oppose the wreckers for many reasons. But, primarily, because, in their desire to destroy profit, they are profoundly unrealistic.

He switches off the machine.

Scene Thirteen

This scene is played on a bare stage. The set cleared during the song.

Why Should We Trust Them Now

SONG:
There is a plot to undermine the nation
To smash all those who smack of
  moderation
Conspirators
Behind closed doors
Their aim
Is total domination.

Chorus:
So why should we trust them now
Why should we trust them, and how
Why after all
When they're way above the law
Why should we trust them now
Why should we trust them

Enter RACHEL.

RACHEL: Rachel. Next morning, I went to see the Federation of Employers. Negotiating Equal Pay. Which, in the Rag Trade, is a kind of joke.
First of all, they trots out the parlous state of the industry. We say, sorry, brothers, law of the land.
Then they pull out the old equal work bit. Take pressing, what they do is put a spring on the press, claim it makes them easier to work. Well, we told them they could stuff that.
Finally, they comes across with the truth. Look, darling, one says to me, look, you can have all the Acts of Parliament you like, you can stuff the statute book, but if you got one and a half million unemployed, people are going to be that desperate for work they'll take it, equal pay or no equal pay. Law or no law.
Well, one thing's certain. One thing it does prove. We got to protect ourselves. No-one else is going to.

RACHEL *joins in the song.*

SONG:
Their purpose is to undermine production
Their tactics are deliberate disruption
They couldn't give a damn
They're wreckers to a man
We're stuck
Till we can bring them to destruction

Enter MICKY.

MICKY: Micky. Next day, went down the dock. Began to work it out.
Well, first thing: Docks Bill's dead.
I mean, this half a mile means nothing. All we fought for, back in '72, that's lost.
And second thing, the dockers dropped, since then, from 42,000 down to 26,000. Promises. Assurances.
And third, in Preston, Council wants to close the dock and sack the dockers. Jack Jones said that if they ever tried to send one docker down the river, be a National Strike.
You noticed it? This national strike? A million words, did nothing. But we smashed it in five days. Protect ourselves. 'Cos no-one else is going to.

MICKY *joins in the song.*

SONG:
Their efforts are too easily discounted
Their sinister campaign's already mounted
Their minds are closed
And those who oppose
Them now
Should stand up and be counted.

Scene Fourteen

*Lights fade to a red glow. Two figures
enter, either side of the stage. We see one
of them first. It's HUDI.*

HUDI: Hudi. That night, walking home.
Through empty streets. Along dead
wharves. The red glow growing
brighter. Then I turned the corner, saw
the warehouse burning. Warm.

*The light grows a little. We see the
other figure.* LINDA. *They don't look
at each other during the dialogue.*

LINDA: Like fires. Come out and see it.

HUDI: Know how it started?

LINDA: Arson. They burn them down,
when they got preservation orders on
them.

HUDI: Who?

LINDA: The companies as owns them.
They employ an arsonist, just like an
auditor or stockbroker. Do a job.

HUDI: I see.

Pause.

LINDA: Can't blame them, though.

HUDI: Why not? It's criminal.

LINDA: Oh, sure. Criminal. But you got
to bear in mind, environmental factors.
They can't help it, owners of the
companies. It's not their fault.

HUDI: Go on.

LINDA: I mean, you got to look at the
background. Childhood, I mean. None
of our advantages.

HUDI: Oh, yuh, I see. Denied, the
benefit of poverty.

LINDA: Exactly. And deprived, of
hunger.

HUDI: Day after day, their mothers
going off for Bridge Fours, leaving
them with only the au pair for
company.

LINDA: Night after night, their dads
coming home stone cold sober on the
5.15 from Waterloo.

HUDI: And from their teens, or even
earlier, interned in Victorian institu-
tions in which they are trained in the
dreadful ways of their class.

LINDA: Exactly.

HUDI: No surprise they turn out how
they do.

LINDA: Can't blame them.

HUDI: Course you can't.

LINDA: Personally, I blame the system.

HUDI: So do I.

*Pause. Slam. Enter GEORGE, in a
hurry.*

GEORGE: Look, I'm the Journal, d'you
know what started it?

HUDI: Who, not what, mate.

GEORGE: Oh. Right. See anyone?

LINDA: No. You never do.

GEORGE looks round, then rushes out

HUDI: Linda.

LINDA: Hudi.

HUDI: Well, here we are.

LINDA: Here we are.

HUDI looks out into the fire.

HUDI: Wreckers.

Into the song:

SONG:
A thunderstorm begins with just a
shower
To stop them gets more urgent by the
hour
We must not fail
'Cos if we do, they'll
Destroy
Us all to keep their power

So why should we trust them now
Why should we trust them, and how

Why, after all
When they're way above the law
Why should we trust them now
Why should we trust them

End of Play

Music

Song Title	Composer
The Filth	Mike O'Neill
Rag Trade Rag	Mike O'Neill
Technology	Si Cowe
Pickets Song	Si Cowe
Stick Together	Si Cowe
Law Locks Up	Gareth Williams
Tale to Tell Your Children	Si Cowe
Folderol	Si Cowe
The World has Changed	Mike O'Neill
Recruitment Song	Si Cowe
Linda's Song	Harriet Walter
Sob Story	Mike Barton
Scribes	Si Cowe & Mike O'Neill
Who is the Labour Party For?	Mike O'Neill
Why Should We Trust Them Now?	Si Cowe & Mike O'Neill

THE FILTH

WE ARE HERE TO TELL YOU OF OUR RO—LE WE ARE GUAR-DIANS OF THE
WE ARE HERE TO SERVE YOU AS A WHO-LE WHE-THER YOU ARE RICH OR
CHORD

L—AW (AND THAT'S OUR TRADE) RI—DING ROUND OUR MAN—OR IN OUR
PO—OR (ON LE—GAL AID)

Z—CAR OR OUR PAN—DA OR OUR BIKE

WE OB—SERVE A FE—LON NICK AN OR—ANGE OR A LE—MON AND WE

(Slower)

STRIKE 'COS WE ARE THE BOYS IN BL—UE

AND OUR AIM IT IS TO SERVE SOME SAY WE'RE

BENT NOT TRUE WELL PER— HAPS A LIT —TLE

TEMPO ①

CURVED VERSE II
CHORUS
TEMPO ① INSTRUMENT FADE

RAG TRADE RAG

FROM

WHITE—CHAP—EL NORTH UP BRICK LANE FROM

ALD—GATE OUT EAST TO MILE END THE

SIGHT YOU'LL OB—SERVE IS THE SAME IT'S THE

GAR—MENT TRADE SET—TING THE TREND WITH

IN—FIN—ITE PAT—IENCE AND CARE WE ARE

FA—SHION—ING WHAT YOU WILL WEAR FOR THE

EAST END—ERS TRADE IS FOR GENTS AND FOR LA—DIES WE'RE
CASH TILL IS RING—ING MA—CHIN—ISTS ARE SING—ING WE'RE

VERSE II IN STRICT RAGTIME

VERSE III AS VERSE I

TECHNOLOGY

Copyright © 1977 for all countries of the world by Hazy Music Ltd, 9 Ravenscroft Avenue, London NW11 0SA.

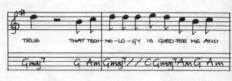

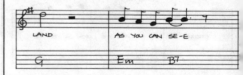

REPEAT INTRO. THEN PLAY VS II. REPEAT INTRO. THEN VS III AS VS I UNTIL

PICKETS' SONG

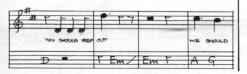

STICK TOGETHER

REGGAE BEAT

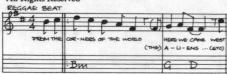

FROM THE COR-NERS OF THE WORLD   HERE WE CAME WEST

(THE) A – LI – ENS …(ETC)

:Bm   G   D

IN-DI-ANS AND I - RISH JUST THE SAME   WHENCE AND WHITHER WE'VE

Bm   G   D   Bm A G   A

– ME   WE'RE ALL OF US FOR-EIGN SCUM. STICK TO–

D   Bm G A / D / † A

GE-THER   TO PRO-TECT OUR-SELVES   SIS-TER   AND

D   Em A   G

BRO-THER   STICK TO – GET-HER   TO PRO-TECT EACH

A   G

VS II CHORUS THEN

[1] O – THER   FROM THE   [2] O – THER

A / A#dim   A / C /

TEMPO 'PICKETS SONG' (6/8)

PICKETS CHORUS (5IVE ARE INSIDE) BUT
AT END 5IVE ARE INSIDE
'COS SPLIT APART THEY'LL DRIVE A …ER ALL OUT
(NB)

D   Am   E9

LAW LOCKS UP

THE   LAW LOCKS UP   THE   MAN OR WO-MAN WHO

B#m C#m T#m / D A E /

STEALS THE GOOSE FROM OFF THE COM-MON BUT LEAVES THE GRE-A-TER

C#m T#m E / E C#m T#m / A E T#m /

VIL-LAIN LOOSE WHO STEALS THE CO-MMON FROM THE GOOSE

E C#m T#m / Bm Bm7 E / A D E

VERSE II UNACCOMPANIED BUT WITH LOWER HARMONY SINGING Vth BELOW (E START); VERSE III + IV AS I

A TALE TO TELL YOUR CHILDREN

VERSE

FOLDEROL

THE WORLD HAS CHANGED

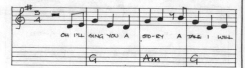

RECRUITMENT SONG

LINDA'S SONG

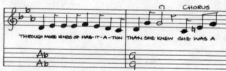

SOB STORY

SCRIBES

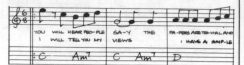

'SCRIBES' IS SUNG TO 'WHAT THE PAPERS SAY' BACKING:

WHO IS THE LABOUR PARTY FOR?

VS III, CHORUS BUT AT END CHORUS AS ABOVE UNTIL:

PAR-TY MAK-ING LAWS THE QUEST-ION MUST BE ANS-WERED RIGHT

C   Dm Em F

N—OW CAN THE PAR-TY CHANGE THINGS ANY—HO—W?

WHY SHOULD WE TRUST THEM NOW?

THERE IS A PLOT TO UN-DER-MINE THE NA—TION TO

F#m   F#m

SMASH ALL THOSE WHO SMACK OF MOD-ER-A-TION CON-SPIR-A-TORS BE-

D   E   D

—HIND CLOSED DOORS THEIR AIM IS TO-TAL DOM-IN-A-TION

F#m   B7   E

WHY SHOULD WE TRUST THEM N—OW?   WHY SHOULD WE TRUST THEM

A   A   A

—NO HOW? WHY AF-TER ALL WHEN THEY'RE WAY ABOVE THE LAW

A   G   G   F#

WHY SHOULD WE TRUST THEM N—OW?   WHY SHOULD WE TRUST THEM

F# E   E   E F

VS II , VS III , VS IV , CHORUS   END OF PLAY

As well as Theatrescripts like this book, **Eyre Methuen** publish a wide range of modern plays and theatre books. Authors include Jean Anouilh, John Arden, Brendan Behan, Edward Bond, Bertolt Brecht, Howard Brenton, Shelagh Delaney, Max Frisch, Simon Gray, Peter Handke, David Mercer, Joe Orton, Harold Pinter and Wole Soyinka, as well as Buchner, Gogol, Gorky, Ibsen, Jarry, Synge and Orscar Wilde.

If you would like to receive regular information about these and other Eyre Methuen drama books, please write to The Marketing Department, Eyre Methuen Ltd, North Way, Andover, Hampshire. Please say if you would particularly like to be kept informed about future Theatrescripts.